BUILDING WEALTH

Story by Story

by

Jan Somers

Published by:

Somerset Financial Services Pty Ltd

PO Box 615

Cleveland Qld 4163.

Telephone: (07) 3286 4368

Fax: (07) 3821 2005

Email: sales@somersoft.com.au

Web: www.somersoft.com.au

First Released September, 1998
Reprinted October, 2000

Printed in Melbourne by McPherson's Printing Group

Distributed by Herron Book Distributors

Copyright 1998, J.B. Somers of Somerset Financial Services Pty Ltd

A.C.N. 058 152 337

National Library of Australia

Cataloguing-in-Publication Data.

ISBN 0 9585672 0 4

Acknowledgement

I would like to thank my dear friend, partner and husband, Ian, for his continued support and enthusiasm. Thanks must also go to my wonderful, patient children, Will, Tom and Bonnie, for enduring the countless hours while I was mostly physically, but often mentally, absent in writing this book. Thanks also to Jenny Somers for all her assistance and suggestions and to Robyn Heales, my editor, for turning my written thoughts into readable English.

About the Author

Today, Jan Somers is just your average millionaire housewife. Twenty years ago she was just your average high school mathematics teacher, who left the blackboard behind to raise a young family. With her teaching career on hold, she took advantage of her time at home to pursue other interests, namely property investment.

Jan's interest in property can be traced back to 1972, when she and husband Ian bought their first house. Although they accumulated many investment properties over the following years, it was not something that was planned.

Constrained somewhat by the needs of three very young children, it was a time Jan used most productively to read and to learn. Introduced to a personal computer for the first time by programmer Ian, she relished the opportunity to analyse investment property in depth, playing with the figures to her heart's content.

At first she had trouble believing what the computer kept telling her, but no matter which way she looked at it, the answer always came out the same: *residential property, properly financed and kept long term, was a wonderful investment!* Jan now had an insight into why the family had been able to achieve so much through investment in property in the past, on just average wages, and for the most part, a single average wage. As a result, Jan and Ian went on to buy many more investment properties and now have a multi-million dollar property portfolio.

Jan never did go back to teaching high school mathematics. In 1989, with Ian, she established Somerset Financial Services Pty Ltd and now enjoys sharing her knowledge with others through her lectures, books, videos and computer software. Her first three books *Manual for Residential Property Investors*, *Building Wealth through Investment Property* and *Building Wealth in Changing Times* were all best sellers, with more than 300,000 copies being sold.

Her firm's Property Investment Analysis (PIA) computer programs have become industry standards, and are now used by thousands of investors, accountants, banks and real estate groups throughout Australia and New Zealand.

Jan's new book, *Building Wealth Story by Story*, is a fascinating collection of stories about fellow investors. But it also contains several stories relating to Jan and Ian's own experiences, with the final story, "My way", providing readers with an insight into the way they have varied the basic "recipe" of property investment to suit themselves.

CONTENTS

Introduction

I have always believed that the best source of information on property investment is other property investors. Following the publication of my earlier books, I was inundated with letters, phone calls and taps on the shoulder, from people who had more questions to ask or stories to tell about their own experiences with property.

I started to think that collating these stories into another book would provide a wonderful opportunity for property investors to learn even more from others.

It is a pity that our education system does not teach people how to manage their financial affairs. The emphasis is on learning skills to earn money, not on money-management skills which can lead to long-term financial security. Consequently, when people decide to invest in property they find they sadly lack knowledge of the financial aspects of property.

So who do you turn to for help? If we turn to the financial advisory industry for information, we often find they give scant attention to direct investment in residential property as their advice is usually structured around managed products.

Who else is there? Bankers? Accountants? Solicitors? As I have said previously in *Building Wealth through Investment Property*:

You can't rely solely on the advice of the bank manager who just handles the money, nor the accountant who does the sums and keeps score, nor the solicitor who ensures you keep to the rules. You should be seeking the advice of experienced, successful property investors.

With this in mind, I decided to compile a book of stories and began to make notes on scraps of paper which I filed in my bottom draw. By 1997, the drawer was overflowing with bits and pieces of hand-written notes and I found that I had so many great stories to choose from that it was a far more difficult task than I had ever imagined.

Instead of sitting down to write, I spent much of the time cutting and culling to select those stories that I thought would have the greatest impact and provide readers with the best possible material from which they could learn. The result was this book, *Building Wealth Story by Story,* which is a collection of stories about the personal experiences of more than one hundred property investors.

Some of the stories will warm your heart. They are about ordinary people doing unordinary things to achieve a goal of financial independence. In contrast, other stories may make you squirm, but I feel they were equally important so that readers might learn from other people's mistakes. You can read this book from "go to woe", or simply open it up and read any section or story that takes your fancy. But no matter how you read it, I know that story by story you will learn from the myriad of experiences of other people.

I don't think any of the stories in the book has portrayed a situation where someone has done everything right. In fact, I know that many of the people whose stories I have used felt they could have achieved more, or achieved it sooner, had they learned the basic principles of wealth building much earlier in their lives.

What *are* these wealth building principles? The property investment strategy that I espoused in my earlier books was very simple, and is exactly the same today as it was then and will be in the future. It is:

1. Buy income-producing residential investment property that is appropriately financed to achieve maximum tax benefits while you are still working.

2. As property values, rents and wages increase with time, continue to purchase property by refinancing so that your liabilities (your borrowings or debt) increase with your assets.

3. At retirement, reduce your liabilities by selling a property or two, or by gradually winding down your loans. This ultimately should provide you with a retirement package of residential properties that should continue to grow in value and produce a regular indexed income.

While many of the stories that follow suggest that successful people have mirrored this strategy, many have discovered and skilfully used the principles long before I ever put pen to paper and long before we ever bought our first property. Like me, they also never learned about property investment as part of their formal education but discovered the principles from yet other property investors, through personal experience, or from books.

My wish in presenting this book is that in reading it, you will identify with those people who have been successful and learn from them. But I also hope you will learn from those who haven't, by understanding the reasons why.

I thank the hundreds of people who generously donated their time in sharing their stories with me and apologise to those whose stories have not been included for lack of space. To protect the identities of those people who have contributed, the names, occupations and locations have in some cases been changed.

1
Take responsibility

I have always believed that as individuals, we are fully responsible for our own destiny in life. As I wrote in my earlier book, *Building Wealth through Investment Property*:

> All too often we put the responsibility for our well-being in the hands of other people and then blame them when things go wrong. Shifting the responsibility for our woes seems to appease our conscience, but it rarely solves our problems.

Today, with welfare budgets around the Western world being slashed, we cannot rely on governments to provide for us in retirement. Australia has an ageing population and by 2020, it is estimated that more than 20% will be over 65 years, compared to 12% now. Clearly, future pensions provided by governments can only get less. Couple this with the 1996 Census findings that the median retirement income is already a pitifully low $8,300 per year, and we have a bleak outlook for those who believe "she'll be right" and consequently do nothing.

If we want to retire in comfort and with dignity, then, we must take responsibility for our own financial future. Many of the stories in this book are about people who have already realised this. I have decided to begin, however, with a group about people who have either failed to accept this responsibility, or have perhaps unwittingly failed to prepare for their future, or have watched helplessly as others have failed. These stories highlight just how easy it is for people to take the soft option of doing nothing about their future financial independence.

1. Gunnas

Several years ago I spoke to a frustrated real estate agent who had just taken a young couple on an inspection tour of investment properties. He was complaining that they'd just spent six hours looking at 27 properties and now they wanted to wait six months until after Christmas.

"Patience," I said. "They're spending a lot of money and they're quite entitled to look carefully at what they're buying. If you just give them a little more time they'll respect you for it."

"A little more time!!" he said, raising his voice. "I'll tell you just how much time I've already given them. Nikki and Judd first walked into my office two years ago, really excited about buying their very first investment property. They told me they'd already been to a lot of seminars and had read heaps of books on the subject and now they were ready to go.

"Well, we spent the next twelve months looking at properties — units, flats, houses, townhouses — the lot. But there was always something not quite right. It was either too big or too small. Too old or too new. Too expensive or too cheap. Too noisy or too quiet. Too shady or too sunny. I won't go on. I even asked them for a list of what they were looking for — how big, how many bedrooms, how old, how much. And when we finally found one that fitted their list perfectly, the mossies were bad.

"One year and one hundred properties later, they rang to say their only daughter was getting married and they would have to put things off for a year. I thought I'd seen the last of them. Then this morning, almost two years to the day since I first met them, they pop into my office and tell me the daughter's settled and they're now ready to buy. So we've been looking all day and now they tell me they're going to wait until after Christmas.

"Now you know why I'm here tearing my hair out. I tell you, they're just gunnas. Gunna do this and gunna do that and they never do."

I smiled. "Yes, they're gunnas."

Author's note:

It's quite OK to spend a lot of time looking for investment property and it sometimes takes a few months of looking every other weekend to find one that suits. It's also quite acceptable to read as many books as possible and to attend as many investment seminars as you can. But at some stage, you have to make a decision and act.

Nikki and Judd always found an excuse not to buy. The properties were never quite right or the daughter's wedding got in the way or Santa Claus came to town. And according to the real estate agent, it wasn't as though they were going to invest in shares or anything else. Unless they make a decision and do something, they will always be just gunnas.

2.   The blame

I met Giles at a private function recently. He was a very disgruntled property investor who, once he learned I was an author who promoted the idea of property as an investment, proceeded with a long-winded diatribe that described his predicament. I knew I was in for an ear bashing when he uttered his first few sentences:

"I question your philosophy on building wealth through investment property. In the fifteen years to 1993, we had good capital gain on our house. But in the five years since, all our capital has evaporated."

Giles continued his story and it became clear that in his eyes, property had been a terrible investment and successive governments and the attitude of the banks had largely been responsible for his downfall. You can make up your own mind as to who was to blame.

In 1978, at age 18, Giles inherited $15,000 from the estate of his late grandmother. At the time, he worked for a large communications company as a technician, and although his income was relatively low, he was able to borrow an additional $10,000 to purchase his own home for $25,000.

In 1980 Giles married and soon after, he and his wife started a family. Though his wage stayed modest, Giles was a good provider, taking on all the responsibilities that go with being a husband and father. He made sure that his young family enjoyed the comforts of a new car and furniture and he even extended their house. Ironically, it was the increasing value of the family home over this period that enabled Giles to increase his borrowings in order to purchase such items.

By 1990 the family had upgraded to a new $150,000 brick home with more new furniture and another new car. By now, however, the original $10,000 loan had crept up to $100,000.

In 1993, at 33, Giles was retrenched, something for which he still blames the Federal Government of the time and the recession "we had to have". He received a $50,000 redundancy package and, with a loan of $150,000, he bought a retail business consisting of two small shops at the end of a strip shopping centre.

Giles leased one of the shops to a TV repairer and set up his own tele-communications outlet in the other, specialising in mobile phones. He believed his 15 years experience in the telecommunications industry would stand him in good stead to run his own business, as he thought he knew everything there was to know about mobile phones. After all, he was rated one of the top technicians in his previous place of employment.

However, the move did not turn out the way Giles might have liked. The recession was affecting retail sales in both his and his leased shop. To make matters worse, he was losing business to the bigger chain stores as a result of the deregulated trading hours that had recently been introduced by the State Government. Gradually he fell way behind with his loan repayments for both his house and his business.

By 1995 his financial situation was becoming desperate and the bank refused to extend his overdraft, having done so four times previously. By the end of that year he was forced to sell both his shops at a loss, and not long after, the bank foreclosed on his home, which was subsequently sold. The proceeds from the sale of the properties failed to cover the debts and Giles was left with nothing. He is now receiving unemployment relief and living in rented accommodation.

During our conversation I could see that Giles was both devastated and bitter. He blames the Federal Government for supporting rationalisation of the telecommunications industry which resulted in him losing his job. He blames the State Government for the deregulation of trading hours and their lack of support for small business. And he blames the banks for not being more sympathetic to individuals in financial trouble.

But he also contends that if property is such a good investment, he should have been able to sell the shops at a profit, which would have enabled him to keep the family home.

Author's note:

What went wrong? Giles questions the viability of building wealth through investment property. But I think his bitterness has somewhat clouded his vision of what really went wrong.

Giles was fortunate to be given a head start with an inheritance, but at no time did he ever invest in property. Purchasing his first home with the help of his inheritance was absolutely the right thing to do. But then he used its increasing value to buy consumer goods to satisfy his "wants" rather than his "needs", and this is where his problems began. Had the increasing value been used as collateral to purchase an investment property, Giles would have been much better placed financially when unfortunately he was retrenched.

As for the two shops, they were never an investment in property so much as the purchase of a job. Investment in commercial property has the potential to produce much higher returns than residential property, but these come with much higher risks.

In general, the fortunes of a commercial investment property are very closely tied to both the fortunes and business acumen of the tenant. And, although Giles may have worked in the telecommunications industry for 15 years and known everything there was to know about mobile phones, he had no actual experience in running a business.

3. Cheap rent

Quite often at seminars I relate snippets of stories I've come across to enhance a point I'm making or to bring the subject matter to life. One such story involves the tenants in our first investment property which, at the time, we had decided to manage ourselves to save money.

In the early stages the rent remained static, until eventually it fell far behind the market rates. Every year that passed (10 years, I might add) I resolved that when the tenants left I would raise the rent. But this was not to be. The tenants were firmly entrenched in our cosy little house and had no intention of moving — and indeed could not afford to. Catch 22! It was rather fortunate for me that they went to live with their son and daughter, otherwise they might still be my tenants paying $30 per week. After this experience, I resolved to always use a property manager.

At the end of a seminar, a woman came up to me and said:

"I really liked your story about the tenants, but I can go one better than that! We had an almost identical situation with the tenants paying next to no rent. They eventually did move out but at one stage, we almost had them back again." And so Justine told her story:

"We bought our first investment property 15 years ago and I decided to manage it myself to save money. We had a middle-aged couple as tenants and I felt sorry for them, being in their fifties and renting. The wife was devoted to their dog and the husband did a few odd jobs around the district. But for the most part, they relied heavily on unemployment benefits.

"They often talked about how they would be much better off if only they could find a cheaper place to rent like a housing commission house. Mind you, they already had the cheapest rent in town and it looked likely to stay that way. I had got myself into a real rut like you did and found it hard to put up the rent.

"They also relished the day when they would be old enough to qualify for the age pension, as they believed this would make it easier for them to get something with the housing commission.

"But whenever I mustered up courage to write a letter about putting the rent up, within hours I would receive a phone call from a finance company questioning me about the financial status of our tenants. This happened to me on four separate occasions and they always asked the same questions:

'For how long have you known Mr and Mrs Frankston?'

'Five years,' I'd reply.

'Mr and Mrs Frankston have just taken out a hire purchase agreement on a new refrigerator.' At other times it was a TV, lounge, and stereo.

'Do you think they represent a good credit risk?'

'Well, they've been tenants of ours for five years now.' Then it became six, then seven, then eight years. 'And they have always paid the rent on time, so in answer to your question, I suppose yes.'

"So there went my rent rise on hire purchase goods and I had to tear up each of the four letters I had written to them about raising the rent.

"They had been there for almost ten years when I received a phone call one evening. They had been battling for some months to keep up with their rent and decided to apply for a housing commission house now rather than wait until Mr Frankston turned 65. He informed me that as they were now both nearing 60 years of age, they wouldn't be able to afford private rental accommodation for the next five years and they needed a reference from me to enable them to apply to the housing commission.

"Two months later Mr Frankston rang me to say they had qualified for assistance, but there would be a three year delay in obtaining a housing commission home. And the only way they could jump the queue was if they lived in a caravan for a minimum of twelve months.

"So they moved out of our rental house and into a caravan to help them qualify faster. We got new tenants, this time using a property manager, and at last were able to increase the rent, and never thought any more about the Frankstons.

"Two years later, we received a phone call from Mr Frankston. He told me that everything had gone according to plan. They had stayed in a rented caravan for the full twelve months and were granted a housing commission home almost immediately.

"But the only house available was a one-bedroom unit, 15 kilometres away out in the western suburbs with no backyard, no extra room for their daughter to stay and visit them, no close shops, no public transport to speak of and no dogs allowed. So they were forced to send their dog to their daughter's place almost 200 kilometres away. By any remote chance, was our house available for rent again, he asked.

"I felt so sad for them. They had waited for so long and put up with so much to qualify for a housing commission home and then they suddenly realised that the Government wasn't going to look after them in the way they had hoped."

Author's note:

This story highlights the plight of many people, particularly those who have relied on Government welfare most of their lives and have become totally dependent. The Government does not have enough money to look after people in a manner they would like. We must all take responsibility for our own future and recognise that governments can only act as a safety net — and one with holes in it, at that.

4. All alone

In 1994 I was asked to present a talk to more than 500 defence force personnel as part of their in-house preparation for retirement. Not that many in the group were approaching 65 years of age — the average age was more like 40, the reason being that most recruits join the defence forces in their teens, complete their 20 years of service, then leave. The purpose of the in-house retirement planning was to help these "retirees" set themselves up financially when they rejoined civilian life.

I soon realised from the questions I fielded that barely a handful in that room of 500 had even begun to think about their financial future and most, when they left, would be starting from scratch.

There was a pervading expectation that the defence forces would look after their personnel for the rest of their lives, even in the "afterlife" — after they had left to join the "real" world. So it was a real joy to receive a letter very soon after this talk from Neville, who had already started an investment plan for himself and his wife Debbie. He wrote:

My wife and I are both young members of the RAAF. As a benefit of being service members we are provided with cheap housing for about $70 per week. We decided we would be silly not to take advantage of this and use our incomes to purchase some investment properties.

Many recruits stay for twenty years and leave with absolutely nothing. But I wasn't going to be like that. I had to pull myself away from their way of thinking and do the best I could for my family. The RAAF has been pretty good to us with the cheap rent and medical bills being paid, but it isn't going to go on for ever.

I had heard my parents say many times that they should have bought this house or should have bought that land, but they never did. And they shrugged their shoulders when I asked why they didn't. So we started to do things our own way which was a lot different to anyone else here.

We are not highly paid. I earn $28,000 per year gross and my wife Debbie earns $27,000. We currently have one property valued at about $160,000 with a principal and interest loan for $120,000 at 11% variable interest. This property has a DHA (Defence Housing Authority) lease for ten years. And we have just purchased our second investment property for $120,000 with a loan of $105,000.

These two properties were obtained in just two years — starting with nothing. Even though we have quite a substantial negative cash flow on the properties, we are very comfortable. We have found that if we had to, we could afford the current repayments even if the properties were vacant.

We don't have a lot of equity in the properties at the moment but we're thinking of putting more money into the loans when we can. Do you think we should pay just the minimum monthly payment, or more than is required, to gain more equity? I'm not even sure that buying investment properties before our own home is the right thing to do. What do you think?

There's a lot of things we don't know and there is no one to ask at the base. No one else here seems to save any money and I think something should be done to help the really young ones who come here straight from school. They have really expensive stereos and cars and spend the rest on a good night out, over and over.

We didn't have much help from our accountant either. He didn't know much about negative gearing or the expenses we could claim. This was probably because he was used to dealing with defence force people who don't have much in the way of investments. With no one else to talk to, any advice would be a help.

Author's note:

Neville and Debbie have overcome one of the hardest problems in life, swimming against the tide of popular belief. With so many people around them going in the opposite direction, it must have taken courage.

In relation to their question on buying investment property before their own home, the answer is the same for anyone in this situation. Buying an investment property is always better financially than buying your own home, purely because of the tax benefits. And if your own rent is cheap or subsidised, the financial advantages are twofold. However, it's a good idea to pay off the loan on your first property as quickly as you can, even if it is an investment property, to have an equity base to build on.

I recently contacted Neville and Debbie to see how they were getting on. They now have two children and have shifted to a different base. They did do things their way and used all their spare money to pay off the loans.

As a result of their increased equity and with lower interest rates, they have bought a third property and still have money to spare for another two. In fact, the rent from their three properties already exceeds their interest bill, providing them with a positive cash flow.

Meanwhile, Neville's friends are asking, "How can you afford to have three properties and two kids?"

These same friends may soon be asking what happened to the pension.

5. The car dealers

Sol and Bert have been friendly rivals for more than thirty years. Sol owned the Ford dealership in a large country town, and diagonally opposite the same road intersection, Bert owned the Holden dealership. Every year for as long as they could remember, both had been nominated by the local Chamber of Commerce as "Local Businessman of the Year".

As well as the local awards, they each regularly won their respective dealership awards for the state. It was obvious to everyone that they were both very successful business people who between them employed more than thirty people from their local community.

Though fierce business rivals, they were very good friends and often played golf with each other on Sundays. They regularly lunched together at the local hotel where they would spend hours discussing the weather, the economy, government policy, the local council and even business tactics. They also talked about family, but never personal finances. They didn't need to. In Bert's eyes, Sol had to be very well off, and in Sol's eyes, Bert had to be well off. And being in the same business, they each knew the kind of money that the other would be making. Heaps.

They lived in the same upmarket part of town, drove the top cars in each range, and were always seen at the best restaurants. On several occasions, their families even holidayed together.

In 1991, within six months of each other, Bert and Sol retired. The car dealerships were taken over by "new blood", as they described it, but they still continued their regular lunchtime meetings at the local hotel. Their conversations continued about the weather and the economy and about the progress of the two car dealerships.

Within two years, however, Bert stopped coming to their regular hotel lunches and didn't play golf on Sundays any more. Sol eventually rang to inquire about his friend's health, believing he must be ill, but it took several phone calls to find him because Bert had moved house. He had sold his upmarket home and bought in a much cheaper area just out of town. In the course of the conversation, Bert bemoaned to his friend that things were beginning to get financially tough since he had retired. He didn't have any real income except from the pension and he was curious to find out if Sol was having the same problems.

"No," Sol replied, "I still get a good income from the dealership." Bert couldn't believe this was possible, thinking that it had all been sold, until Sol explained. "I still own the land and the new dealer pays me rent."

I first met Sol when he approached me after a seminar with a query on whether or not to sell his land with the car showrooms. It was then he told me this story and how he had fared so much better than his friend Bert simply because he had bought the land "all those years ago". But now you know *what* happened, I should fill you in on *how* it happened. Or better still, in Sol's own words:

"When I started selling cars from the site back in 1960, I was leasing the land. There was only a caravan on it at the time and I decided that if I was going to pour any more money into the place, I'd better buy the land. So I made an offer on it for $10,000. That was a lot of money back then. I could have bought five houses in town for that price. And then my wife and I struggled with the loan to build the showrooms a few years later.

"I never ever knew what Bert was up to then. But he always seemed to have more money to flash around than me. We holidayed together, except that he stayed a few weeks longer than us. He'd also go overseas without us once a year. And I noticed he had the most expensive set of golf clubs.

"I didn't know until recently that he never owned the site. But me and my wife, we always knew we had a solid investment beneath us for when we retired.

"Bert and I often talked politics and he was always complaining he was paying too much in taxes to pay for the bludgers in society. Now he's on the other end of the scale and barely getting by on a pension. Not that I'm saying *he's* a bludger or anything. Far from it. He worked hard all his life. But now he tells me that after paying all those taxes for all those years, he thinks the Government should be looking after him better.

"He's not wrong there. He paid a bundle in taxes. But he should have realised a long time ago that he was never going to get it all back for his pension. I feel sorry for him, but I can't do much, can I?"

Author's note:

That wasn't Sol's real question, but I could see that Bert's predicament played heavily on his mind. His real question was whether or not to accept an offer of $1,000,000 he had just received for his land and showrooms. He currently receives an annual rent of $120,000 but he was wondering if he should sell up and buy several residential properties so he could off-load one at a time if he needed money in the future.

Quite frankly, I didn't have an answer to either of Sol's questions. Firstly, it was clear he couldn't do much to help his old friend Bert who is just too bitter about the Government to even think about helping himself. And secondly, Sol's commercial property is very high-yielding, with a sound tenant in a business that Sol knows back to front. It was also bought pre-capital gains tax. But the point of the story was really not to solve Sol's problem. Sol's problem is a real nice one to have. Bert's isn't....

2
Follow your dream

One of my favourite musical albums is called "Follow Your Dream", written by Shay Healy and sung by the Irish singer Daniel O'Donnell. The lead song on the album is all about making dreams come true:

The road we walk is long and lonely,

And you only get to live one life,

So if you've a dream that you believe in,

To make it real you may have to fight.

It is quite often necessary to jump hurdles, change direction or, as Shay puts it, "fight" to follow your dream. Daniel O'Donnell had a dream of becoming a successful singer but chronic laryngitis almost stopped him. He overcame this to be the most successful country/easy listening singer outside of the United States, and explaining it very simply, he has said:

"I have followed my dreams — and my wildest dreams have come true. I would never have imagined so many dreams fulfilled."

All successful people have dreams. If you want to be successful in any aspect of your life, including your financial future, you too must dream and then set goals to fulfil those dreams. Otherwise there is no motivation to achieve anything beyond where you sit today.

In my travels giving seminars around Australia, I have encountered many people who have achieved the seemingly impossible by following their dreams, but I have also come across people whose dreams have been shattered because they lacked the strength to follow them through.

6. Towards Sydney Harbour

Ben and his wife Liz are family friends whom I have known for many years. Originally, they came from a small country town near Tamworth where Ben was a brick layer and Liz his labourer. In 1975, not long after they married, they built a house for themselves there for just $12,000. But ever since their honeymoon in the big smoke — Sydney — they had dreamed of the day they could own a house on Sydney Harbour. Their plan was to get there one step at a time, no matter how long it took.

In two years they had paid off their loan and decided it was time to move on, one step closer to their dream. So they bought a house further down the coast in Newcastle, keeping their country house and borrowing the entire amount for this next property. They both worked long hours re-establishing themselves in their new area.

In 1981, with their second loan paid out, they made their next move to Gosford. Again they borrowed the lot while retaining their two earlier properties. This move was their most difficult. The building industry had slowed down and it took three years of heartache to rebuild their business. Nevertheless, they were determined. They still had their goal of living on Sydney Harbour and if anything, the dream was even more vivid.

In 1985 the building industry was in such a bad way that Ben and Liz decided to keep themselves busy by building another home for themselves in Mosman. They built the garage first, moved in, then built the rest of the house, relying solely on the rent from their three earlier properties. And they took a good look at the Sydney market.

They realised that many houses in Sydney would have great views of the harbour if only they were higher. So they created a market niche for themselves, which proved to be highly successful, erecting second stories on top of existing houses. This not only gave the owners harbour views, it added more space.

In 1993 Ben and Liz fulfilled their dream. They bought an old house in Balmain on the waterfront with views across the harbour to the bridge. They borrowed almost $500,000, keeping their four other properties that had allowed them to proceed one step at a time to their house on Sydney Harbour.

Author's note:

Liz told me they could have done things better because they always had a tax problem, with no debt on their rental properties, yet large debt on their own home, that was not tax deductible. But as she said, "Tax wise, we did everything topsy turvy, upside down and back to front. But hey, who cares. We achieved what we wanted to and got where we wanted to go — Sydney. So who cares?" It's hard to argue with that.

7. The dream home

Les and Emma, a Brisbane couple, wrote to me in 1996. After reading the first few paragraphs of their rather lengthy letter, I thought that their story was going to turn out to be the same as quite a few others that I had heard or read over the years — about a young couple striving to get their dream home. But half way through, I realised this was very different. In fact, their story resembled one I had just finished reading in Jeffrey Archer's book *A Twist in the Tale*.

We are a hard working couple in our mid-forties who started with nothing in 1976. We dreamed of one day owning our own home on a large acreage and had a plan to work our way up. Our intention was to buy old places, live in them while we renovated and then sell at a profit so we could go on to buy bigger and better each time. Eventually, we believed, we would get our dream home.

Our first property was an old Queenslander on stumps, and my husband, they called him the mower man, worked underneath the house fixing mowers. The house was very rundown and we slept in the dust and dirt for almost two years before we were able to make it presentable. Then we sold it and bought another dump.

Five years and five renovations later, our dream came true. We moved into a house on a large acreage which cost us $200,000 — four times the value of an average house at the time. My husband set up a huge work shed for his mowing business and we were just ecstatic. We continued to work hard, and in a short time we paid off the small loan we had on the house. From then on, we spent all our spare money adding to the house and yard. It was like a bottomless pit soaking up every cent.

Then we started a family. This was the best thing we ever did as it gave me time to stop and think. Before the kids, every minute was spent head down, bum up working on the house. But after my two children were born, I was forced to spend more time inside where I could hear them if they cried. It was just too hard to start painting the shed, only to find I'd have to run back inside to screaming kids.

So I used what little time I had between kids' feeds and sleeps to read. And I started to think about our finances for the first time. For the past five years we had thought about nothing else except pouring money into our home. And for a while I even dreamed of buying an even bigger house on even larger acreage. But I soon realised we needed to invest for our future. We decided that since residential property had played a big part in getting us where we were, then that was the way we would go.

Most people would find it hard to believe what we did next — we actually sold our dream home. Our friends couldn't believe it. It was 1988 and we sold it for $300,000 (there was at least $100,000 worth of blood, sweat and tears in it by then) and we bought four properties, one to live in and three as investments.

We paid cash for our own home and two of the properties, and took out a small loan for the third. The three investment properties were new and we got tenants for them immediately through an agent, but the one we moved into was just awful. After living in luxury for the past few years, it was hard going back to living in squalor. The only concession we made was that this house was also on prime acreage, but the small shack was a far cry from the 30 squares of luxury we'd had before. So we started the process all over again. This time, we got tradesmen in to help. I didn't mind living in a dust bowl for a few months, but not for a few years!

A year later we had turned our dust bowl into a magnificent home — and then we sold it. And with the tax free profits we were able to buy two more properties: a new one to rent out and an old one to live in. And off we went again. We had a two part plan where we bought and renovated our own house and sold it, then ploughed the profits into more investment property. We did this three more times, buying and selling our own home.

I am pleased to say we are now back where we started thirteen years ago. Well, not quite. We have just moved into a large house on 12 acres — our second dream home. But instead of having just one dream home as we did before, we now have our dream home plus seven investment properties.

Author's note:

Les and Emma had the courage to change the course of their dream for the better. In retrospect, they realised they could have had their dream home *and* their investment properties too by borrowing against the equity in their home at the beginning. But as Emma pointed out when I rang her just recently about publishing her story, they were prepared to work on their own home and add value so that they could build up equity even more quickly by making tax free profits.

It is hard to find a compromise between how much money to spend on your home (which is better than spending money on cars or boats) and how much to invest. Many people live in their dream home and spend all their money on it to make it even better, but have no investments. Though at the other end of the scale, why would you live in a caravan and have fifty investment properties? Where is the happy medium? Only you can decide.

8. Stolen dream

Jean is a single mum bringing up two teenage children by herself. Her husband left more than 10 years ago, leaving her with a hefty mortgage on the unit she continued to live in. After the divorce Jean decided to make a good life for herself and her children, and vowed not to have to rely on social security. She got a job at the local supermarket and through careful budgeting was able to pay off her mortgage in nine years.

Early last year, Jean spoke to me at one of my seminars in Sydney and told me excitedly of how she intended to buy an investment unit in the same block of units as her own. Having lived there for many years, she knew the units were in a great position and that rarely were there any vacancies in those units that were rented. The asking price was $180,000.

She told me the agent thought she'd be able to secure the purchase for $170,000 because the owners were anxious to move south to live closer to their adult children and so were keen to make a quick sale. Jean was just so enthusiastic about the unit that she had already arranged with her local bank for the finance.

Jean had done her own sums, too, and had calculated that if she fixed the interest rate at 7.6% for five years, her loan repayments of $13,000 per year would be mostly covered by the $8,000 net rent and her $3,000 tax refund.

She said at the time that although she wasn't good at sums, being a sole parent had forced her into learning to do budgets. And so when she left at the end of the seminar, she was in such high spirits that it even made me feel excited for her.

A year later, Jean came to another seminar I was doing in Sydney and told me how she was just about to buy another unit. Remembering her from the earlier seminar, I expressed delight at her progress believing that she now had acquired two properties.

"No," she said, "this will be my first investment property. The other sale fell through."

"You mean you couldn't get the finance?" I said disbelievingly.

"No, the finance was OK."

"The vendors decided not to sell?" I was curious.

"No, I decided not to buy."

Then she related the tale of how she had stalled when it came time to sign the contract on the unit she had set her heart on.

When she was just about to purchase her first investment property Jean's self esteem was sky high. She was on top of the world, until....

Until her "friends" at work began to undermine her confidence. They all wanted to offer her free advice.

"You've just paid off one loan, why would you take on more debt?"

"But I didn't think the banks would lend money to a single woman."

"Won't you need a guarantor for the loan?"

"You'll be 60 by the time you've paid out the loan."

"Isn't it time you spent some money on your kids?"

"If you get married again, your new husband mightn't like it."

"Your ex-husband could come and take away all you've worked for."

"I wouldn't have my tenants living in the same unit block as me."

And on it went. Jean received such a whirlwind of advice from her "well-meaning" friends that she reneged on the deal. She told the agent she just couldn't go through with it. She had pen in hand and was ready to sign when her imagination got the better of her. Maybe the friends were right. She didn't want to be paying off a debt when she was 60 and she didn't want to let her kids miss out.

For a year, Jean lost sleep over what she hadn't done and slowly came to realise that her friends had stolen her dream of standing on her own two feet and becoming financially independent. Not only had they stolen her dream, they had cost her more than $50,000. In just one year, the Sydney property market had increased the value of the particular unit to $220,000.

Jean has since bought a unit in an adjacent street and is now well on her way to achieving her ambition. Her friends are still her friends, but she now has the courage to stand by her own convictions.

Author's note:

How many times have well meaning friends and rellies put you off doing something that you firmly believed was right for you? How many times have you said, "I wished I hadn't listened to them. I wished I'd made up my own mind"?

These people often do honestly believe you might get out of your depth in waters unfamiliar to them. There undoubtedly is an element of concern for you on their part.

But if you have done your homework well, there should be no reason whatsoever why you should come to grief. It would be far better for those helpful folk to encourage you to move ahead and then prop you up if you look like you need it — which is rarely the case.

Remember, the majority of the population retire on an average income of $8,300 per year. If you want to be one of them, listen to what they say. If you don't, stand by your dreams or they may be stolen.

9. The present

I met Keith and Donna at a seminar in Sydney in 1992. They were just a young pair in their teens who wanted to know about buying a house for their Mum and Dad. (I found out later as we were talking that they were brother and sister, aged seventeen and sixteen.)

Their mother did piece-work sewing at home and their father was an invalid pensioner confined to a wheelchair following an accident for which he'd received no compensation. Keith left school when he turned 17 to work in a local hotel and Donna left soon afterwards to work as a waitress in a Chinese take-away.

They had a dream that one day they would be able to help their parents to buy their own home. Five times in the past eight years the family had been forced to move when the property they were renting was sold. It was traumatic every time, and so they desperately wanted to buy a house to protect their parents, particularly their father, from this.

I told them very simply that they had to set aside a certain amount from their incomes each week and save a deposit. With the incomes they were currently on (Keith was earning $14,000 per year and Donna $11,000), I suggested it could take them five to ten years. But they obviously had other ideas about how long it would take.

"How can we make it happen sooner?" they wanted to know.

"If you're prepared to do it, you'll need total commitment. You'll have to forgo everything, and I mean everything, and save every cent of take-home wages and buy only the barest essentials."

Two years later, in 1994, Donna rang to say they had just fulfilled their dream, and she told me their story.

They had made a pact to start saving immediately, but they had no illusions about what the home would be like. Forget the timber kitchens, the ensuites, the extra garages and the plush carpet. Any low-set house (because their father was in a wheelchair) anywhere would do.

They decided to make an all out effort to save as much as they could each week. Both walked to work to save on bus fares; they never went to the movies or bought new clothes. Their only entertainment was sport. Keith played football and Donna netball. And Donna's boss regularly gave the family left-over Chinese meals.

Their mother was very supportive, even though she thought it was a hopeless idea as they had never owned anything before — even the TV was on hire purchase.

Almost unbelievably, after eighteen months, they had saved $20,000 between them. Their expenditure in that time, apart from tax, totalled just

$6,000, and most of this was spent on either paying off the refrigerator and TV, or rates and power.

With their $20,000, Donna and Keith approached their local building society where they had been saving for that year and a half. They had worked out they'd need to borrow about $60,000 to buy an $80,000 house they had already chosen on the outskirts of Penrith. The house had no floor coverings, no built-in wardrobes and only one kitchen cupboard under the sink.

The manager was very sympathetic to their cause but unfortunately, he told them, for legal reasons it was impossible. Donna was only seventeen and a half at the time and was too young to be registered on the relevant legal documents or to have her income included in a loan application. And Keith's wage alone was not sufficient.

With no other income that could be considered (their father's pension didn't count and neither did their mother's income as it was intermittent and unreliable), their request for a loan was denied.

Still determined, Keith and Donna decided to wait another six months and then try again, which they did, and this time their application was approved. By then they had saved almost $30,000, an incredible amount considering it had taken them only two years, and on very low wages.

They found another low-set house in the same area for $80,000, paid a $25,000 deposit and borrowed $55,000. With the remaining $5,000 they paid the stamp duty, etc., and bought a few items of furniture. The home, as Donna described it, was not everyone's idea of a dream home. It was a very small three-bedroom house with just the basics, but it was the best present their Mum and Dad had ever had.

Author's note:

Today, four years after buying the family home, Donna and Keith owe just $10,000 and should have the loan paid out by the time this book goes to print. And they have every intention of buying more property — this time for themselves.

Saving for that first deposit is perhaps the hardest, but it is the most important step in building wealth through investment property. For it is then that the saving and spending habits become firmly part of a way of life. It requires total commitment, but Donna and Keith have shown that no matter what income you are on, it is possible, it can be done. There are really no excuses.

Perhaps it isn't necessary to go to the extreme lengths that Donna and Keith did, but the principles of setting a goal and chasing a dream are exactly the same.

10. The dream boat

In May, 1994, I received a letter from a young man who wanted to build a boat. Bruce worked in a North Queensland coal mine out in the middle of nowhere and lived in a single men's camp — which makes it a bit difficult to understand why he would want to build a boat. But Bruce was someone with a mission, as you will gauge from his letter.

I am writing to you in relation to your book and the reality that has come about through real estate. A small book and video tape were handed to me about three years ago. They talked about becoming a millionaire through property investment.

I immediately put up a mental barrier, thinking I would have to miss out on too much fun in life to achieve this status. So I gave myself 20 years to do so. I have long since returned the book to its owner, but I have followed the principle you wrote about.

After buying my first house over the phone at a single men's camp at a North Queensland mine, I became enthusiastic. I became interested like in a hobby. I began to read. I set goals and achieved them. My biggest hurdle was to realise the simplicity of it all, but once I overcame this, I excelled myself. I have not yet reached year three and if I carry on doing this and if I continue at the rate I am going, I will become a millionaire in under five years, through your principles. I have blown my own 20 year limit to bits.

I have been overseas twice, travelled down to South Australia and up to Townsville. I also fly to Brisbane whenever I want. I eat only the things that are good. I exercise regularly. I look after my body and my soul.

I attend the four-monthly gradings at Rockhampton for Yun Jung Do. I attend the yearly Yun Jung Do seminars in Brisbane and I have just now completed an Alpha Dynamic course in Brisbane. I have also successfully completed a Coastal Navigation Diploma Course through correspondence in readiness for when I build my boat. I donate on a regular basis to many charities to help people less fortunate than myself. All since I bought my first property.

Do you think I have missed out? I don't think so.

I have chosen to use the power that God entrusted to me at birth. The power to choose, to be free. Freedom to be what we choose to be is the equal right of everyone as long as what we do benefits other people as well as us. Jan, thank you for showing me the way so I can pursue further goals in my life. I have reset my retirement age to 43. And it is my dream to be in command of my own relief support vessel helping Islander people in the South Pacific region. I did not know how I was ever going to get there but through your book, I can now clearly see the way. I intend to keep on buying investment properties until I fulfil my dream and build my boat.

I give you full permission to use this story in any of your books or lectures as I hope it will help other people to fulfil their dreams.

Author's note:

I don't intend this story to be a testimonial for my earlier book, but this letter from Bruce was one of the most stirring I have received over the years. He had obviously set his goals high and his dream of building a relief boat to sail around the South Pacific would surely have been beyond comprehension to his mates at the mine. I kept the letter to one side for a long time, often wondering how Bruce had fared and hoping to use it one day in a book such as this.

When the time came to put Bruce's story to print, however, I was very hesitant about ringing him, because many of the Queensland mines had since closed down. I eventually decided that his letter was so positive he would surely have succeeded in the face of any adversity. So I rang.

I was most relieved to find that he was still at the same address, with the same phone number, and even more relieved to find that he had done exceptionally well with all his property investments. I could have rapped myself on the knuckles for even daring to think any negative thoughts. I, of all people, should have had a much more optimistic attitude.

In fact, Bruce had done so well that he had achieved more than he said he would. He had blown his original goals apart. Bruce's philosophy was to buy the worst house in the best street and rent it "as is". He collected many run-down properties, all in good locations, and has now begun to demolish many of them to replace them with blocks of units.

As well as his property investments performing exceptionally well, his personal achievements have also been of note. He now holds a black belt in Yun Jung Do. But best of all, Bruce is close to achieving his ultimate goal of taking his own support vessel on relief missions in the South Pacific. He has completed the necessary navigational courses and is having plans drawn up for his dream boat.

When we last spoke, he had just returned from a trip to China to oversee the final design stages of the plans and was now negotiating with one of the island governments in the region about building the boat with local labour. Bruce estimates that by the end of the year he will have fulfilled his dream of being in command of his own relief boat and will be helping people less fortunate than himself. He is indeed an inspiration to others.

3
Start when you're young

We can all look back on our younger days and regret that we wasted money on things that gave us instant gratification when we could have been saving for our retirement. Perpetual Funds Management reported in their survey of people and their retirement intentions that most recognised that they didn't start early enough, "and nearly a quarter of those surveyed hadn't started at all".

How early is early enough? According to social psychologist Walter Mischel, perhaps as young as four. He implemented what is known as the marshmallow test where four-year olds were given the choice of receiving one marshmallow prior to doing an errand, or two if they could wait until they had returned. The implications of this experiment were reported by Daniel Goleman in his book *Emotional Intelligence*:

> Which of these choices a child makes is a telling test; it offers a quick reading of the trajectory a child will probably take through life.

Most people who succeed financially are those who in their younger days delayed gratification and started saving. Not only did they have the advantage of having an entrenched savings pattern early in life, but they gained the magic benefits of compound growth over a long period of time.

The following stories are of people who started investing in property when they were young. But don't despair if you already have a few grey hairs and haven't even thought about investment yet. The good news is that self control and investment planning can be learned. And as the next chapter will discuss, it's never too late to start.

11. Going places

Three years ago I received a letter from Alexander, who was obviously a young man going places. The letter was not about financial tactics, nor techniques to buy property. It was about pure determination and it gave me a lift just reading it. I hope it does the same for you.

I am only 19, but I know exactly what I want in life and I know that I will get there with or without the help of others around me. For the past year I have thought everyday about the goals I have set and the dreams I one day will achieve. I believe that anyone can do anything they want to if they want it badly enough.

I am currently working as a waiter in the hospitality industry, and I'm moving rapidly up and up and on line with my career plan. I see myself in perhaps five or seven years owning and operating my own hospitality establishments.

I also love real estate, and I think that I will be able to combine the industries fairly easily. I find that when looking at properties I see things I can improve or change and ultimately make money from. I don't own any property yet but I soon will — that is for sure.

At the moment, I'm still living at home, saving as hard as I can. I am very ambitious and determined and I will make a success of my life. That's not an issue because I know I will.

Ultimately I wish to be a multi-millionaire and I want to buy nice things for my parents, and to be able to give them a long holiday in Scotland, where my mother was born.

Thank you for listening to me.

Author's note:

I rang Alexander recently to see how he was getting on. His mother answered the phone and it was clear she was very proud of her son.

She told me what a diligent worker he was and how he loved his work. He always started early, finished late and rarely had enough spare time to even think about wasting his hard-earned money. He was still living at home and had progressed to being the assistant manager at an exclusive, award-winning restaurant.

Alexander then came to the phone and completed the story by telling me that he had already bought his first unit and was about to buy his second. As if on cue, within another four weeks he wrote to say the deed had been done. He had just bought his second investment property!

Watch this space for a young man going places!

12. It's easier now

A few months ago, when I was cleaning out the spare room at my elderly aunt's house, I found a cache of letters. My aunt was a prolific letter writer and had accumulated letters from friends all over Australia. She suggested I might like to read them as some were very interesting and many dated back more than fifty years — and there was nothing too personal in them. So I did.

One letter in particular, written this year, was about property. My aunt and her husband had owned quite a few flats over the years and she was very interested in property. This letter from her friend Ivy, who lived in Melbourne, was about the ebb and flow of property affordability over the years. The letter was obviously prompted by Ivy's own daughter's battle to buy a property. Ivy was a very astute seventy year old and I reproduce this letter so that young people will understand that buying a home today is no more difficult than it was 40 years ago. And in many respects, it is easier.

Buying a house has never been real easy, but when today's couples complain about the deposit gap and the high cost of housing, they should remember that 40 years ago the situation was much the same, if not harder back then. But somehow people managed.

When I married in 1959, my husband earned $1,900 a year as a bus driver and the cheapest brick house we could find was $7,600 on a new estate. Finance was not a problem, but we found it hard to save the $1,000 we needed for a deposit. This was, after all, more than six months wages.

In 1979 in Victoria you could buy a similar, but much better equipped house to the one we bought, for $39,000. The wage for the job that my husband did was then $13,000. A house cost three times a year's salary, not four, as it did back in 1959, so in a way you could say things were easier in 1979. And the deposit was $6,000, which was less than half a year's salary.

Today, in 1998, my daughter and her husband want to buy a house and we have been trying to tell them it is just the same now as it was when we bought in 1959, and if anything, easier now. The cost of such a house today is $145,000, and my son-in-law, who is a courier driver, earns about $36,000 per year.

So the cost of a house is now four times a year's salary, the same as in 1959, but the necessary deposit is only 10% of the house price ($14,500). And they should be able to save for this much quicker than we did. So in a way it is easier to get a house now in 1998 than when we did in 1959. I don't honestly know what they are complaining about.

Author's note:

I checked out the figures in Ivy's letter and the property prices and wages she mentions are all spot on. The property prices are a touch below the median price of houses in Victoria at each date, and the wages are almost identical to the historical average male wage data provided by the Australian Bureau of Statistics.

I would like to have referred to the Housing Affordability Index, which is the official measure of the cost of borrowing to buy a house relative to average wages, but unfortunately this has only been calculated in more recent times. Consequently, the chart below is simply a reflection of the observations my aunt's friend made, looking back over almost forty years. But it shows that in terms of the deposit needed and the cost of a house relative to salary (i.e. the affordability), it really is easier to buy a property today than it was forty years ago.

Home affordability

	Property Price	Salary	Price times salary	Deposit required by bank	Deposit as % of property	Deposit as % of salary
1959	$7,600	$1,900	4	$1,000	13%	53%
1979	$39,000	$13,000	3	$6,000	15%	46%
1998	$145,000	$35,000	4	$14,500	10%	41%

From this table you can see that the deposit required to buy a property in 1959 relative to the average salary was quite high at 53% of salary. And back then, the banking system was rigid in its requirements for home loan lending. Getting started would have been the hardest part.

By 1979 the cost of a property relative to salary was less, being just three times the average salary of the day. And the deposit required as a percentage of salary at 46% was less than in 1959. The real problem then was that there was a credit squeeze in the late seventies and finance was not readily available. When it was, interest rates were high.

Today, in 1998, the cost of a property relative to salary is the same as it was in 1959 but the deposit required relative to either the cost of a property or salary is low at 10% and 41% respectively. And with the deregulation of the financial markets, money is readily available with home interest rates at an all-time low of around 6%.

As I said, my Aunt's friend was very astute. She would no doubt find it as strange as I do that the proportion of high-income young people owning property has fallen in recent years. (*Trends in Home Ownership* by Dr Judy Yates)

13. Too young

Greg wrote to me in 1991, detailing his property acquisitions over the past 12 years. When I recently dug out his letter I saw something stapled to it that I had not noticed before. I had to ring him to find out about it.

In 1979 Greg attended Tech College as an apprentice electrician. At the college library he saw a book by Fred Johnson and Brendan Whiting called *The Way Ahead To Property Wealth*. The book struck a chord and at just 18 years of age Greg bought his first property. Over the years, he knew what property he wanted to buy and how to finance it, but he hit one small problem. Most agents thought he was too young to be taken seriously.

On one particular occasion, when he was 22, he walked into a real estate office and told the agent he was looking to buy a block of three or four units. The agent said he'd keep an eye out for such a property and would get back to him the minute something came up.

A few weeks later Greg saw an advertisement in the local paper for a block of four units, exactly what he had been looking for, advertised by the same agent he'd recently spoken to. When he rang to find out why he hadn't heard about it, the agent said he'd thought Greg was too young to be serious about buying property and was just big-noting himself. Greg decided to do something about it and produced his own business card that looked like this:

Greg Court   Property Investments
*Purchaser of Houses, Units
& Blocks of Flats (any condition)*

Ph (123) 24 6802

**53 The Avenue
Timber Flats 1234**

Greg has used his business card ever since to introduce himself to real estate agents, who now ring him if they think they have a property even vaguely suitable, tradesmen, who are now very prompt at giving quotes, and financiers, who now come to him.

Author's note:

Greg's young friends all laughed at his business card, but nowadays he is laughing all the way to the bank. He now has the latest in home office equipment with a computer, E mail, fax and mobile phone to help him oversee the large portfolio of properties he has built up since. Now you know how Greg got started, you can read more about him in Story 97.

14. Follow the son

When I was first told this story by a bank manager friend of mine I thought it would make a very interesting story about how parents could best help their children. Then I realised it was really a story about how children could best help their parents.

David started saving for his first car when he was barely 13 years old by doing odd jobs around the neighbourhood. He spent weekends and his school holidays mowing lawns, painting fences, and he even did the shopping for one elderly couple. In four years, he had saved $10,000.

On leaving school at 17, David got a job as a labourer with a builder, a man he had mowed lawns for, who was impressed by his work ethic. By his 18th birthday he had saved $15,000, but at the urging of his boss, he had become more interested in buying a house than a car. He approached his local bank and was told that while his income would support a $90,000 loan on the $100,000 rental property he had put a contract on, his $15,000 was not enough for a deposit plus all the extras. His options were to wait another year to save more money or use some other property as security.

"Would your parents be interested in helping out?" David was asked.

He didn't want to ask his parents for money, but they turned out to be very keen to help and decided to mortgage their own home to enable him to secure the loan. By this, they could help David without actually handing over any money, and they had enough confidence in him to "not get into trouble" with the loan.

Within two years, David had paid off almost $30,000. His parents were so impressed by their son's commitment that they decided to follow in his footsteps and buy an investment property for themselves. They approached their bank, only to be told that because their own home was already mortgaged (by David), they needed to wait a few years to save for a deposit or use some other property as security.

This sounded familiar, but the bank manager quickly came up with another alternative. David had so much equity that the bank could shift his mortgage from his parent's home solely on to David's property. This would free up the family home allowing David's parents to use it as collateral for an investment property of their own — which they did.

Author's note:

I wouldn't recommend you mortgage your home to just anyone: David's was a very special case that highlights one method parents can use to help their children. I'm sure there are many more. The story also highlights how children can take the initiative and set an example in investing that their parents may follow.

15. The forklift driver

In my book *Building Wealth through Investment Property* I talked about the misbelief that to become wealthy, you need a highly paid job. I related the story of a forklift driver who left school at 15 years of age and had never earned more than the basic wage in his life, yet he owned 47 town houses and had just bought a jet aircraft. This story aroused many questions and comments from readers, such as:

"I find that story just a bit hard to believe. Is it true?"

"Is he really just a forklift driver?"

"Are his properties located all over Australia?"

"I presume he is married and they both work!"

"Does a real estate agent manage his business or do he and his wife?"

"He must have been buying properties for a really long time!"

"I would appreciate it if you could tell me more about that person!"

So to satisfy reader curiosity, here is the story about Len, the forklift driver. But I'll let you in on his little secret now. Len simply started buying properties when he was very young, aged 18, in 1953 and never looked back.

Len's family emigrated to Australia in 1948 from the then Soviet-controlled Latvia when he was thirteen and his sister eleven. They came with a dream of starting a new life in a new country free from oppression.

Len's father was an aircraft engineer who could speak Latvian, Russian, Czech, German and Polish, but not English, so he was forced to work as an unskilled labourer in a printery, relinquishing his skills as an engineer. Len's mother worked as a domestic at one of the hospitals.

Within a month of starting school Len left to join his father at the printery, and with three family members now working they saved enough over the next three years to pay cash for a house in South Brisbane.

This was late 1950 and the three-bedroom house with verandahs front and back cost £1,500 ($3,000) through the estate agency of Noonan and Knowles. It was very rundown and on a busy road, yet Len remembers how jubilant his parents were when they first moved into their "castle". He decided there and then to do the same for himself.

For the next three years Len continued to work at the printery and was able to save enough for a deposit on his first property. It was 1953 and he was just eighteen and finance was hard to get. No bank was willing to finance a young unskilled labourer.

Len searched the papers for a property in which the vendor was willing to leave money. He eventually found one, a one-bedroom, old house in

West End (an inner suburb of Brisbane) for £850 ($1,700). But the vendor requested a further £50 ($100) in cash on the black market for the privilege of leaving £300 ($600) in the house, to be repaid within two years or the house would be forfeited. Len's father came to the rescue with the additional money and Len had bought his first house.

With the help of the 45 shillings ($4.50) in weekly rent on top of his wages Len repaid the loan in a short eighteen months. He was terrified that if he didn't pay it back quickly he would lose the house altogether.

In 1956 Len bought another property which he eventually moved into with his wife when he married later that year. This property became the family home where Len and his wife raised their four children.

Between 1956 and 1991, Len continued to work for the same printing company, while his wife stayed at home to look after the children. During this time the couple bought another twenty properties, all run-down houses on large blocks of land in and around the inner south side of Brisbane.

Len called them "penny dreadfuls", his term for describing his style of investment property, but he kept his properties well maintained by doing all the repairs himself. His policy was to save a large deposit each time he bought, so that the rent covered the loan repayment. Then he paid off the loan as quickly as he could, using the rents from his earlier properties to make inroads into the loan even more swiftly.

In 1991 Len decided to demolish half of his houses, the ones on land zoned medium density. He then borrowed to build 47 brick townhouses on those sites, something his father had been urging him to do for many years. Len's father's is a story in itself, as he eventually went on to become a very wealthy businessman involved in the construction industry.

And the jet aircraft I mentioned? Not long after selling his first batch of penny dreadfuls Len sold a few more to buy a run-down Learjet for him and his father to play with in their old age. Len only recently retired from his job as a forklift driver at the printery to spend more time tinkering with his plane.

Author's note:

Len has achieved so much in his lifetime. Not because he did anything special with his properties, or was particularly lucky, or had a high income or even a double income.

In part, Len's success arose from the fact that he learned to save and enjoy the simple pleasures in life at a very young age, a result of the vivid memories of living in an oppressed country. But most importantly, he started when he was young, only 18 years of age, and benefited from the magic of compound growth over more than forty years.

4
Never too late

A survey recently asked people their attitudes towards investment. The reason was government concern that too few people were investing for their future. The most common responses in the age groups were:

18 - 24   Too early to start investing. Will do it later.

25 - 44   Too busy with kids and mortgages. Will do it later.

45 & over   Too late to invest.

The fact is, it is never too late to start investing. And with the old age pension as we know it under increasing pressure, anything you do at any age will make you significantly better off than having done nothing at all.

In 1982, Walt Jones was a guest on the Johnny Carson Show. It was his 110th birthday and he was explaining how he refused to accept age as a barrier to doing anything. While describing how getting old was not such a big deal, he said:

"As a result of a little condominium investment I made a few years ago (in 1978), I've made more bucks since I was 105 than I did before."

As I said, it is never too late to start investing and it is never too late to start buying property. Age is a state of mind, and with life expectancies ever increasing, Ben Gurion's prediction that we might all live to 100 is fast becoming a reality. Even at age fifty, we could well have another fifty years of active life left. Of course it helps to start investing in property when we are young, but the following stories should give heart to all who believe they have left their run too late.

16. I'm 65

Bart is 65 and has just retired. He has been looking forward to the day for a long time, having worked as a watchmaker for a large jewellery chain for the past fifty years. He faithfully paid into his work's superannuation scheme throughout, even boosting his contribution in the last three years to improve his final payout.

But when the day dawned, Bart realised that his $200,000 payout was only going to provide him and his wife with an income of around $10,000 per year, supplemented by a small part pension. The payout figure was no surprise, the problem was what it meant in terms of his future income, as explained to him by a financial planner. And to make matters worse, all the company blurb about the importance of having superannuation had led him to believe he would be well off when he retired.

Bart told me when he rang that he'd have done something about it years ago if he'd imagined he could be in this predicament. He'd had numerous opportunities to invest in "lots of other things", as he put it. If only he'd known his super wasn't going to be enough.

"But now it's too late," he said. "I'm 65, and I'm just too old to do anything now. I might have bought some property forty years ago if only I'd known. But in a few years, I'll be 70."

"But how old are you really, Bart?" I asked.

"I told you, I'm 65," he repeated as though I was deaf.

"No, I mean, you're 65 on paper. How old do you feel? Is your mind old? Is your body old? We all have this 65 mentality. It's a huge mental barrier. And then we start thinking about being 70, as you did, and then we think about dying. The fact is that we are all dying from the moment we are born and there is no reason why you can't do now, what you might have done forty years ago."

I didn't continue with my psychoanalysis of age and he went away to think about it. But he obviously got the message, as two weeks later he rang to say he had been offered a part-time job three days a week with the same jewellery company. And he had bought three investment properties with his superannuation money and a small loan that the rents now cover.

Author's note:

I couldn't count the number of times I have heard of people who have suddenly found themselves with a superannuation payout that falls far short of their expectations. And it is not the amount that surprises them, but how much it means in terms of income. As a very simple rule of thumb, you should aim to retire with assets of 20 times the income you think you will need in retirement, all in today's dollars. Will *you* have enough?

17. The country vet

Harry and Sylvia lived in a small country town in Victoria and were its best known identities. Harry was the local vet, and had been so for forty years. He had built up a very busy and successful veterinary practice, with a client base stretching for hundreds of kilometres around the district. They were always perceived as "well-to-do" and they spared no money in living up to that image, attending all the functions, balls and parties, and they even had a racing carnival named after them.

Over the years, their circle of friends came to include both top business people and famous politicians. And the more they socialised, the bigger their network of acquaintances grew and the more clients they attracted to their veterinary business, and so it went on.

The climax to their socialising came with the marriage of their only daughter to a Melbourne doctor. It was the biggest social occasion ever to occur in the small town and was talked about for years later. The event lifted Harry and Sylvia to even greater social heights.

They always planned to retire when Harry reached sixty and constantly kept their eyes open for good investments. Many opportunities did come their way, mostly from their own veterinary clients who regularly offered them "the investment opportunity of a life time". These included a pine plantation, an ostrich farm, a crayfish farm, an ultra-light plane school and a native Australian flower farm. All promised to make Harry and Sylvia wealthy by the time they retired.

Harry and Sylvia weren't totally gullible people. They could see that some of these ventures might be "pie in the sky". However, it wasn't easy to say "no" to important clients who generated much of their veterinary business. Saying "no" also had the potential to undermine their social standing in the community. So they "invested" in some of these local enterprises, believing that if they hit the jackpot with just one, they would be set for life.

But as Harry neared sixty and began to look more closely at his many investments, he realised they were all worthless. He saw they had bowed to social pressures far too often and had not taken the initiative themselves. Even worse, after ploughing in hundreds of thousands of dollars over the years, they were in debt for $150,000, a legacy of having mortgaged their home for one of these ventures.

Harry was overcome by a despair he couldn't shake off so it was left to Sylvia to try to resurrect their future. She consulted every financial advisor she could, even travelling to Brisbane and Sydney. It seemed to her as though everyone was offering to take charge of their finances, but she was very aware, after their experiences, of what could happen if they lost control. She thought she might do better talking to people who had been very successful with their own investments, and quickly realised that the most successful people she knew were her own daughter and son-in-law, who owned a lot of investment property in Melbourne.

Their daughter had watched her mother and father put their money into dubious schemes for years, but was always extremely reluctant to interfere in their financial decisions, so she welcomed the opportunity now to help them set up a retirement plan.

Between the four of them, Harry, Sylvia, daughter and son-in-law, they mapped out a ten year plan which involved Harry continuing to work — not such a burden as he loved it — paying off their mortgage, and buying as much property as they could meanwhile.

In two years of concentrated effort they whittled their mortgage down to $50,000. In that time, they also found it remarkably easy to ignore the many "business opportunities" that continued to come their way. Even more surprising to them was that they didn't lose any clients by declining, and likewise didn't lose any friends. Harry kept wishing he'd learned to say "no thank you" to these propositions years ago.

It was now time to start stage two and they went ahead and borrowed to buy their first investment property in Melbourne for $130,000. They weren't very keen on taking an interest-only loan. They wanted things to happen fast. So they took a principal and interest loan and proceeded to repay it as quickly as possible.

Harry is now 65, and when I last spoke to his daughter they had five investment properties and were still going strong. They also have a whole new outlook on life and retirement is the farthest thing from their minds.

It was Gloria, their daughter, who told me this story five years ago at a Melbourne seminar. She wanted to know if I thought it was too late for her mother and father to be starting to buy investment property, with them both already over sixty. So I reiterated to her my conviction about investing in property — it is never too late.

Author's note:

Harry and Sylvia are typical of what can happen to people who bow to the social pressures associated with living in a small community where everyone knows each other and what everyone else is doing or not doing (or so they think).

They poured their money into risky business ventures for fear of losing friends and clients. These kinds of social pressures are very difficult to overcome and require a strong sense of commitment. It is important to take the initiative and commit to your own investment plans. Then it is easier to decline others.

18. Mod-cons

I received a phone call late one Sunday night at about 10 p.m., just as the Sunday night movie *Witness* with one of my favourite actors, Harrison Ford, was coming to an action-packed finish. The caller, Marvin, excitedly wanted to tell me he had just finished reading my book *Building Wealth through Investment Property* and it was the answer to his dreams.

Even though I wanted to get back to the movie I persisted with being polite, believing it would be just another one of those thirty second complimentary calls which are always nice to get, though preferably not at 10 o'clock on a Sunday night. But Marvin went on, despite my subtle silence.

"I'm tired of living out here in the middle of nowhere. I'm nearly fifty and for twenty years I've lived under a leaky roof, with no running water, no hot water, no TV, no microwave, no stove, no washing machine and I only have lights on if I can stand the noisy generator. In fact I don't have any mod-cons other than this phone, but now I'm going to have everything I want. Your book has shown me the way to my dreams."

"I'm pleased Marvin, but...," and before I could finish he was off again.

"Yep, all those rents from all those properties will do it for me. I've always dreamed about getting out of here and having a nice home and all the rest." And he repeated himself. "And all those properties and rents are the answer to my dreams."

I was beginning to realise he was building castles in the sky. But I don't like to sound pessimistic and I hate the idea of killing off anyone's dreams, so I decided to stay with it. I had already missed the end of the movie.

"Marvin, how are you going to buy all these properties in the first place? You'll need to actually buy properties before you can get any rent."

"Easy," he said, "just borrow the money and I'm off."

"Yes, but you'll need either a deposit or some equity in your own home before you can do that," I warned him.

"No problem, I have $37,000 to start with," he said.

"Do you mean you have $37,000 in cash, or $37,000 in equity?"

"No, my home here where I live is worth $37,000."

"What sort of home is it?" I asked, trying not to sound demeaning.

"Its a nice little home on about 100 acres," he told me, "but I'm tired of having to drive so far to the shops and I'd really like just a few mod-cons."

It was time to ask some crunching questions so I could get to bed.

"You might have enough equity to buy one property, Marvin, but you'll also need an income to service the loan."

"No problem," he replied. "I get $200 a week from Social Security."

The picture was now complete. Here was a man, living in a shack, hundreds of miles from nowhere, with no income to speak of, no cash and none of the modern comforts he craved for.

"I'm sorry," I said, "but you need a real income to start an investment plan and later on, when you've built up a portfolio of properties, you can have all the comforts you want. That's the way it works."

I'm not sure why I persisted after this but as I said before, I try to be optimistic rather than pessimistic, so I offered him a few suggestions.

"Look, Marvin," I said. "You're going to have to get yourself a job. Then you can go to the bank and find out if they'll mortgage your property so you can borrow against it to buy something else. Then, if you keep on buying properties, eventually you'll be able to retire on the rent and buy all those appliances and things that you've dreamed about."

"Oh," he sounded almost sick. "So I really do have to work. But I'm nearly fifty. Isn't it too late for me?"

"Yes, you do have to work, and no, it's never too late. Let me know how you get on, but maybe you could ring me between 9 and 5 in the day, not between 9 and 5 at night."

"I'm sorry," he said, "did I wake you up? I don't have a clock. I'll be ringing you as soon as I can."

And he did. Five years later I had a phone call from Marvin. He had sold his shack and easily found himself a job as a fireman in the city, having been a member of his country fire brigade. He told me:

"When I got to the big smoke I found a room I could rent cheaply, and it's got a lot more comforts than I had at the old place. Then I used my money from the acreage that I sold as a deposit on an investment property which cost $100,000, and I've almost paid it off. I'm just about ready to buy my next one."

"Marvin," I said enthusiastically, "that's really great news. I think your story would be an inspiration to others."

Author's note:

It doesn't matter how old you are when you start, but you definitely need an income. There's no other way. I make no apologies for this. I have never pretended we can become wealthy with no effort at all. What I do know, though, is that by working hard and channelling your hard-earned money into investment property, you will eventually be able to afford all the "mod-cons" you ever dreamed of.

19. The taxi driver

I first met Garth in early 1998 when I took a taxi from my city hotel to a seminar in suburban Melbourne. He was the driver. We got to talking about property and what was happening in Melbourne, and then he told me how he planned to retire at forty years of age. I'm not a good judge of age but I reckoned that Garth was already closer to fifty than forty, so I asked him politely how he intended achieving his goal.

"I've already retired, but that was ten years ago."

"So you love driving taxis so much you still drive them even when you're retired?" I asked, thinking anything was possible, because here was I working away at something I love doing (seminars) even though I retired more than ten years ago — *and* working longer hours than I ever did.

"Nope. I'm only back doing it because I ran out of money," and he continued his story:

"When I was a young bloke driving taxis around Melbourne I worked 18 hour days, 7 days a week, so that I could retire when I reached forty. The thought of not driving taxis any more was what kept me going.

"And I was pretty careful with my money. I didn't eat take-away food like most of the other taxi drivers. My wife packed me a cut lunch and I always came home for dinner. My wife put up with a real lot. Sometimes I'd be home for dinner at five and sometimes it wouldn't be until midnight when I'd finished the shift.

"We bought our first home in 1970, just after we married. We didn't stop there: two years later I bought my first taxi licence. I thought I would ease up then and get another driver, but I had learned so many tricks of the trade that my driver wouldn't be making anywhere near the amount of money I could have made in the same time.

"Most of the other taxi drivers would just sit and wait in the ranks for a fare to come along. Some would just do the airport route and sit and wait in a taxi queue for the planes to come in. But not me. I used to read the newspapers backwards — starting with the social pages. Then I knew what was going on in Melbourne every day and night of the week, and I'd go straight to the venues just before finishing time. And not just the big events that every one knew about. Not just the races and the football. Sometimes they were a waste of time.

"The taxi drivers who thought they were smart following the big events would sit and wait all afternoon for a fare. When they finally got one after the game was over, they'd get so bogged down in traffic that they usually only finished up with just the one fare for the afternoon. But I knew when and where all the socialites had their parties. I knew the whereabouts of all the entertainers, not just the really popular ones but the also-rans with a small following who performed at the local clubs.

"I handed my business card to everyone and my wife used to take all the calls and call me on a two-way radio I had installed. I reckon I was the first taxi driver to own a mobile phone and it cost me close to $2,000, but it more than paid for itself in the first month.

"Anyway, you get the picture — real hard working, 'smarter than the average bear' taxi driver with a goal to retire at forty. And my Chinese wife also had this incredible work ethic so while I worked 18 hours a day in the taxi, she worked 18 hours a day at home. She did everything from looking after our three kids to mowing the grass.

"And the story gets even better. After we bought our own home and a taxi licence, we kept on going. Eventually, we bought two investment properties and another taxi licence.

"Kind of as if by magic on the day I turned forty in 1988, we reckoned we had enough to retire. We decided to live in Taiwan, my wife's native country, and it took us six months to sell up everything in Melbourne and move. From the sale of the three properties and the two taxi licences, we must have had close to $500,000 when we moved to Taiwan.

"I can't say exactly how it happened, but within eight years we'd blown the lot. Our kids had wanted to stay in Australia in boarding schools so there were regular trips for them to see us and us to see them. I visited my elderly parents in England at least twice a year. We bought a tiny flat on the outskirts of Taipei for my wife's mother and sister. We liked going to the casinos and eating out at restaurants with all my wife's relatives. Somehow, it all just went.

"So two years ago, in 1996, we came back to Australia to start all over again, and I began driving taxis for someone else. Within a year we had saved up enough for a deposit for a house and I was able to buy a taxi licence from someone who knew me from ten years ago and was willing to accept an IOU for almost the entire $200,000, more than double what I had sold one licence for eight years before that. This time around, our goal is to retire for good by the time I reach 60."

Author's note:

It is never too late to start — even again. Garth did everything right in building up his assets, but he greatly underestimated his retirement needs, in particular, his retirement lifestyle. He found a new freedom, but his lifestyle changed from that of being a spendthrift to a spender. Had he continued to live as he had when he was driving taxis he would still be a wealthy man. But Garth is a very good taxi driver, and I have no fear he will make the same mistake twice.

20. Back on track

Jim and Joan are long-time good friends of ours. They always believed that investing in property was a secure way to go, and even told us about its advantages years before we ever bought our first home, when we weren't ready to listen and learn.

Jim's parents owned a lot of property and had brought up their children to respect hard work and sound assets. So when Jim and Joan married in the late 1960s they immediately built a pair of flats, living in one and renting the other. This, they thought, was a good start in life. They then settled down to hard work to wait for their next chance.

Over the next few years, despite all their good intentions to buy more property, Jim and Joan's priorities began to change. They were trying to establish a business, which needed regular injections of money, and they also started a family, which absorbed any spare money they had. Though they continued to work hard, waiting for their finances to improve, they were only able to focus on their business commitments and family needs.

When the children started school Jim and Joan found their flat was too small. They didn't think they could afford to buy a bigger home in the same suburb, and they didn't want to move out of the area they had lived in for most of their lives. So when the tenancy agreement expired on the adjacent flat and the tenants had moved out, they knocked a hole in the wall between the two flats and expanded their family into the adjoining rooms. They felt as if they were going backwards instead of forwards, however, owning only one residence now, instead of two, and losing the rental income as well.

After almost thirteen years of living this way, they decided enough was enough. Their children were now teenagers and their business had also grown and had taken over one of the bedrooms. So they went in search of a real family home, large enough for everyone to have a bedroom each, plus a home office and sheds for their business, and preferably in the same area as they lived.

They were excited, but at the same time apprehensive. Their intention was to borrow enough upfront to buy a house and sell the two flats later, thereby reducing the bridging loan. This way, they wouldn't have to move twice or rent in between selling and moving into their new home.

They soon found an ideal house, with four large bedrooms, a study for their home office and a large shed for their business equipment, in an area close by. And you wouldn't believe it, but the land was part of a sub-division previously owned and developed by Jim's father more than thirty years earlier. Although it had changed hands many times since, his name was still at the top of the title deed as the developer.

Jim felt it was more than just a coincidence that he should be buying a property that had belonged to his father. He was reminded of his earlier vow — to follow in his father's footsteps.

They consulted their bank manager and found he was more than willing to finance their proposition to buy the house, then sell the flats to reduce the loan. So Jim and Joan signed the contract and moved into their house, still finding it hard to believe that the trees in the backyard were probably planted by Jim's father, decades ago.

Over the next few months, things went even better for Jim and Joan. The house turned out to be fantastic, suiting both their family and business needs; their business picked up, and the flats, which were in the process of being fixed up ready for sale, came up looking really nice, with interest already being shown by several buyers.

In fact, things were going so well that when they sat down to look closely at their finances, they realised that they might just be able to keep the flats instead of selling them. So they went to their bank manager a second time, and he concurred that they could indeed afford to keep the flats, which they did. Three weeks later, with the hole in the wall repaired, the flats were rented.

And so, almost 30 years after buying their first investment property they were back on track. In addition, to help minimise their tax liability, their accountant transferred ownership of the two unencumbered flats to their discretionary family trust, allowing them to eliminate the loan on their new house and negatively gear the flats.

Jim and Joan now have a new lease on life. They love their house on the land that Jim's father developed. But their story doesn't end there. One year later, Jim and Joan bought another investment property! And they are now so keen on the idea that they have encouraged their offsider, who had completed his apprenticeship with Jim more than 10 years ago, to buy an investment property too!

Author's note:

I feel elated when I hear stories like this, especially when you have the opportunity, as I have had, to watch the self-discovery process. Jim said to me just recently:

"I still can't believe it's so easy. To think we started off so well then struggled all that time with our minds shut. That decision to move was the start of a revelation — a whole new world opened up."

The learning path is often long and tedious — in Jim and Joan's case, 30 years. But it is rich with rewards. So long as we have our wits about us, and our minds open, it's never too late to learn and to act.

5
Good debt

The right kind of debt can speed up your quest for wealth. The wrong kind can send you broke. It's really as simple as that. So how do you distinguish between good and bad debt ? It's as easy as asking yourself this question:

"If I buy something now with borrowed money, will it be worth more or less in ten years time?"

In general, if what you want to buy will be worth more in ten years time, then the debt is good. If it is going to go down in value, then the debt will be bad.

Many people don't grasp the connection between wealth and debt of the right kind, and in fact, there is often a misperception that good and bad debt are synonymous with small and big debt. And so a small debt of $10,000 on a car is often mistakenly thought to be better than a bigger debt of $100,000 on a unit. In my book, *Building Wealth through Investment Property*, I explained the difference between good and bad debt this way:

When you next think of debt, think of the following conversation between two young boys.

1st boy: We are so poor that my Dad owes the bank $2,000.

2nd boy: We are so rich that my Dad owes the bank $2,000,000.

An increase in wealth is usually linked to an increase in debt of the right kind, and the following stories are of people who have used the right kind of debt to build wealth through investment property.

21. The symbol

One Sunday morning I was sitting in my office working on this book when I looked out the window and saw our favourite three-seater lounge sitting on the balcony, with our dog Scully sprawled across it. I had been pondering all morning about which one of six stories I would use to fill this particular spot on "Good debt" when I saw it.

To me, this lounge is a symbol of good debt. Now, I know you may have trouble associating a consumer item such as a lounge with good debt. So let me tell you the history of this lounge, so you will understand.

In early 1976 we bought a house in Capalaba, just south of Brisbane. This was our second house, and we had just transferred back from Sydney without a skerrick of furniture. Not that we had ever had any real furniture. I had furnished our first house for just under $300 in 1972 (about $1,800 now) and when we went to Sydney we gave most of it back to the second-hand store where we had bought it.

So when we moved into the Capalaba house we had nothing but our personal belongings and an old TV, which had all fitted into our old car for the trip north. I set about buying furniture, including a second-hand lounge advertised in the local paper for $80. It had a light timber frame with elasticised straps, and thin foam cushions in a faded red floral material which I later replaced.

This lounge took pride of place in our house. In fact, it became a well-travelled lounge, having been in five houses since, and it has even been to Sydney and back again. For more than twenty years we carted that lounge around like a Louis XVI piece of antique furniture.

In that same twenty year period we borrowed quite heavily to invest in property. And the reason we were able to was because we never borrowed to buy furniture, though a new leather lounge like many of our friends had would have been nice. We were up to our eyeballs in debt, but it was the right kind. We were really sitting pretty, you might say, because of our spending priorities.

I'm sure you'll see now why that lounge out on our balcony is, in my eyes, a symbol of good debt.

Author's note:

Did you know that after tax, buying a leather lounge on hire purchase costs about the same as borrowing to buy an investment property? If you want to build wealth, the choice is simple. Later on, you will be able to buy your leather lounge, your new car and anything else you want. We do. But I still keep that old lounge, albeit refurbished a little, on the balcony of our home overlooking the sea as a symbol of what good debt is about.

22. The choice

I met Duncan in Sydney this year when he spoke to me after a seminar. I remembered him well because he came in late — 45 minutes into my talk or 15 minutes from the end, whichever way you care to look at it.

"I'm sorry I was late, but I was taking my wife to the hospital. She's having a baby tomorrow," he rather sheepishly explained. "But I just had to talk to someone about the CGT I have to pay on this property I own."

I told him I wasn't an expert on CGT (Capital Gains Tax) and that he would be best to talk to his accountant.

"I have already. And he thinks I'll have to pay $100,000. In 1994, before I married, I bought a one-bedroom unit at Bondi Beach overlooking the ocean, for $200,000. I was living at home, and with the rent from the unit I paid out the $150,000 loan, and now I don't have any tax advantages. But my real problem is that in the last few years, prices have gone crazy in Bondi and the unit is now worth about $400,000."

"That's a nice problem to have," I said. "Why don't you keep it?"

"Because my wife doesn't want to live there. I'd like to keep the unit, but she wants me to sell it and use the equity to buy a house in Penrith closer to her parents. You know, with the baby. She says we'd be better off to then borrow against our home to buy another investment property so we can get back the lost tax benefits. I can see some advantages in this, but I'd be losing $100,000 cold in CGT. Is there any way around it?

"Not really. But why not keep the Bondi unit as an investment and borrow to buy the Penrith house?"

"I thought of that, but I'd have a $300,000 non-tax deductible loan."

I explained he had a simple choice of paying the CGT or paying more in personal income tax. By selling the Bondi unit to pay for his house he would pay CGT, but then he could save on personal tax by borrowing to buy another investment property with a tax deductible loan. By keeping the Bondi unit, he wouldn't pay CGT, but he wouldn't save on personal tax by borrowing to buy his home with a non-tax deductible loan.

Duncan rang the next week to say his wife had had a son and both were doing well. He also said his accountant had done the sums and thought he would be best to keep the Bondi unit and borrow for his own home.

Author's note:

People sometimes go to enormous lengths to rearrange loans to make them tax deductible, believing that all non-tax deductible debt is bad. But often the costs of reversing the situation far outweigh the tax benefits gained, particularly if there's CGT to pay. Often it's better to focus on repaying the non-tax deductible loan as quickly as possible.

23.   All for $100

Perry and Karen are a young North Queensland couple in their mid-thirties. Perry rang one day to order our investment analysis software which he hoped would confirm what he had worked out by hand.

"We owe $1,000,000 and it only costs us $100 a week. I've double checked the sums and I know I'm right, but I still can't believe it."

And with that simple statement, he went on to tell me how it had come about:

"In 1986 we paid off our first home. We had been waiting a long time for this day so we could go on and buy more property. I know now that we didn't have to wait until we had paid off our home before we could buy again, or we would have started sooner. But I didn't think we could afford to have two loans because our wages were not very high at the time.

"Anyway, the day after we made the last payment on our home loan we went looking for an investment property. It took us a month to find one we were happy with and we bought it for $70,000. The hardest part was believing that it cost so little to buy more property. We kept buying more and more and we now own 10 rental properties as well as our own home, with a total value of $1,400,000. And our debt is $1,000,000. I still can't believe that it costs us just $100 a week!

"We pay interest of $70,000 per year — the loans are interest-only with $700,000 fixed at 7.2% and $300,000 variable at 6.5% — property expenses of $17,000 per year, and we get a tax refund of $7,000 and $75,000 in annual rent. So it costs us $5,000 per year or $100 per week. That's the minimum we need to pay, but we put a lot more towards our variable loan.

"At first, we had to get used to handling big sums of money. The rates bill alone is $4,000 a half year and the interest bill is almost $6,000 a month, and the rent we get is about $1,500 a week. But I thought, if we are going to retire wealthy, we have to get used to dealing with big sums. I'm just a clerk for a hardware store in our town and my wife and I have a bigger turnover of money than the store.

"We know we may not get a large capital growth on our properties because we live in a coastal town, not a big city. But we've figured we only need a small capital growth to make it work for us."

Author's note:

Perry's figures were absolutely correct, but believing that the cost of buying investment property can be so cheap is often harder than buying it. And he is quite right on another point. Learning to manage large sums of money while you are building wealth is part of the process of learning to handle large sums effectively when you retire wealthy.

24.   Monty's rules

I thought I knew everything there was to know about borrowing money until I met Monty. I met him almost fifteen years ago when I thought we were at the limit of our borrowings, but realised we were only at the tip of the iceberg. Monty today is a self-made zillionaire who owns a huge number of properties all over Australia.

For all the property he owns, though, Monty has never injected any capital of his own and has never earned an income from a regular job. His secret was that he learned how to borrow money. You may not agree with how he borrowed it, but it worked, and worked well, and that was all that mattered to Monty.

Monty started in 1952 with £100 ($200) which his grandmother gave him to "help carry her bags" to England. The boat trip didn't turn out as expected and Monty, eighteen, used the money to buy a block of land on the east coast of Victoria, which was all he could afford.

He lived in a tent on the land for a year, clearing it and then buying building materials from a local farmer to erect a house. The arrangement was that Monty would pay double what the materials were worth once the house was sold. The old farmer had nothing to lose as the timber and tin had been sitting on his property unused for a decade. Within eight months, Monty had sold the house and land and repaid the farmer.

Monty immediately returned to Melbourne hoping to expand on his small fortune. He wanted to use his £300 ($600) profit to buy some land or a house in Melbourne — anywhere, and in any condition. After many fruitless trips to the banks, however, he began to despair. Who, after all, would lend money to a young boy (Monty was then nineteen), particularly when he didn't have a job.

It was a chance meeting with a barber in 1953 that changed the tide of fortune for Monty. This barber was the focal point in his community and knew everything there was to know about everybody, including an intimate knowledge of their money. Who had it, how they got it, when they got it, what they did with it, and most importantly, who would lend it.

It wasn't long before Monty secured his first loan, from a local doctor. It was 5% interest-only, when the going bank rate was about 6%, but the upfront fee of 3% was renewable every three months, effectively making the interest rate 17%. Monty found an old house on the northern outskirts of Melbourne, split the land in two, built another house on the spare block and sold off both in less than six months.

For the next thirty years, Monty continued to visit the barber every month. The barber, who was known around town as the "go between", supplied Monty with the names of people from whom he could borrow money. This barber was not only a good barber, he was a good broker.

Monty borrowed from solicitors, doctors, butchers, car dealers, builders, farmers, pharmacists, dentists, restaurateurs, accountants, publicans, timber merchants, printers, photographers, Chinese cooks and even horse trainers, to name just some he could remember. Monty knew the stakes were high, so he set himself some rigid rules by which he played his money game. Monty's rules were:

Never buy shares, just property with borrowed money.

Never borrow money from friends or relatives.

Never lend money to friends or relatives.

Never buy cars with borrowed money.

Never cheat on lenders.

Never tell lies to lenders.

Never have loans fall due at the same time.

Never have all loans with the same lender.

Never delay loan repayments.

Never run short of cash.

Never stray from the rules.

Monty made millions over the years and throughout, he never deviated from his self-imposed rules. When you ask him if he had any rules for buying property as well as borrowing money, he says:

"Do a bit of renovating, a bit of trading, a bit of building, a bit of selling but a bl- - - y lot of keeping."

Author's note:

In the 50s and 60s, credit was tight. Banks were not willing lenders of money and did not pay good rates either on cash deposits. Consequently, many wealthy businessmen were happy to "invest" their money at the exceptionally high interest rates offered by the money brokers in the back streets of Melbourne, and no doubt other cities as well.

Even though Monty's sources of finance were a little unconventional, the rules by which he played are very conservative and are a good model for borrowing money today. Monty continued to borrow from his trusty sources right up until the early 1980s, when the financial system was deregulated. With the subsequent freeing up of the system, money lending became more institutionalised, the bigger banks becoming flexible enough with their lending arrangements to effectively compete with the "backyard" lenders.

25. The commitment

Miles and Tanya own a successful hairdressing salon in Melbourne. In 1980 they reached that momentous occasion of making the final payment on the $70,000 loan on their home which was then worth about $100,000 — an expensive house at that time. They earned about $60,000 per year between them, when the average worker earned less than $20,000 annually.

They worked hard, often into the night and seven days a week. When they weren't cutting hair at their salon they were out at nursing homes, cutting, perming and tinting all the old ladies' hair. With all the hard work, it had taken them just five years to pay out their home loan.

In the ensuing years Miles and Tanya tried to save money to invest for their future. They were very aware they should do something, but most times when their bank account reached $5,000 they spent it. They bought new clothes, jewellery and antique furniture. They rationalised that they worked so hard they simply deserved these rewards.

And if their bank account reached $10,000, by some quirk of nature their car broke down, or their house needed urgent repairs, or there were huge medical or dental bills to pay. It was as if someone knew exactly how much they had saved, because that's how much these things always cost. So no matter how much they saved, it always disappeared.

Their accountant often suggested they negatively gear into either shares or property, but they weren't particularly interested in taking on another loan as they thought they had worked so hard to clear the debt on their home and it might interfere with their lifestyle. They were always needing that money anyway for when things broke down, and they certainly didn't want to be stuck in an emergency.

They told him that instead of borrowing money, they would rather save the excess cash from their hair dressing business to invest in something. But year after year they saved with good intentions, only to find that their savings soon slipped through their fingers. For ten years, Miles and Tanya saved money, only to spend it. Save, spend. Save, then....

But in 1990 Tanya's father died, leaving the $400,000 family home in Sydney to Tanya and her two sisters. Neither of her sisters wanted to keep the property but Tanya didn't want to sell, as the house had been in the family for more than sixty years and she had a special attachment to it. So she and Miles decided to buy out her sisters' shares. They arranged finance for the $270,000 payout and rented the house within the month through a local real estate agency. Tanya takes up the story:

"We were dead scared about taking on this $270,000 loan. It was more money than we had ever borrowed in our lives before. But I wasn't going to let the old family home be sold to a complete stranger. So Miles and I took the plunge and borrowed the money. I can tell you now, it was the best thing we ever did. We should have done it years before, when our accountant first suggested it.

"The strange thing is that eight years after taking on a loan that we didn't plan for, we are heaps better off than we were for the ten years before when we didn't have a loan. And to boot, we've paid out that $270,000 loan completely. I can't explain it except that we saw this loan as a commitment.

"And in that time, we still had our overseas holidays, still bought new clothes and I continued to buy antique furniture. But we were probably just that little bit more careful with our money.

"The really strange thing was that for some reason, nothing broke down any more. Before we had the loan we always had emergencies at the worst possible time, and it used to take all of our savings. I gather this is called Murphy's Law. After, I think we paid more attention to things, and got problems fixed before they turned into expensive emergencies.

"I really don't know the answer. All I know is that before we had the loan, we had no commitment to anything and the money just disappeared. It was just too easy to get to, sitting in that savings account. I could call it Murphy's Second Law: your expenses will always equal your earnings. And it was true. No matter how much we earned, we spent it all.

"I can see now that we probably shouldn't have paid out the loan in such a hurry, because we now pay a lot more in tax. But if we hadn't put the extra money towards the loan, I'm sure we would have spent it.

"We'll be taking out another loan shortly to buy another investment property and we'll probably pay that one out too. Otherwise I know the same thing will happen all over again. No loan, no commitment."

Author's note:

A loan *is* a commitment. It is a commitment to your future. It forces you to put aside money that would in most cases be frittered away — consumed in one form or another — with nothing to show for all the hard work over many years.

There is that old adage that you might be better off with your money sealed in a concrete box buried in your backyard rather than having it in the bank earning interest, the reasoning being that even though you might get a good interest rate on your money in the bank, you still have access to it. But you can't easily get to your money buried in that box metres under.

My husband Ian has his own anecdote. He says the best way to make a carton of beer last longer is to store it in a warm place, not in the fridge.

6
Bad debt

Some years ago the Queensland State Government introduced a home loan scheme called HOME, an acronym for Home Ownership Made Easier. It was intended to give "battlers" a chance to own their own home, as many had trouble qualifying for outside sources of finance.

In talking to a senior public servant about the merits of the scheme, I was told, however, that most HOME applicants didn't qualify for a home loan with a normal financial institution, not because their incomes were too low, but because their living expenses were too high!

For many, living expenses in our modern world have come to mean items we can't live without, from big screen TVs to swimming pools, new kitchen appliances, stereos and four wheel drives. And it was the cost of hire purchase of such items, commonly called consumer debt, that stopped these "battlers" from obtaining a home loan from normal sources.

The escalation in consumer debt can be traced to the introduction of the credit card, appropriately called fantastic plastic, which has enabled people to borrow to finance their lifestyle with great ease. But the joys of instant gratification are short lived. Too much consumer debt will ultimately send you broke.

In fact, debt on any item that falls in value over the longer term is bad debt. This can include debt on investments where the initial capital is lost. The following stories highlight the problems associated not only with consumer debt, but with debt that is used to finance these rather dubious investments.

26. The car

Ten years ago our old car began to die. It had served us well for almost thirteen years but it had got to the stage where there were so many things that needed fixing, it just had to be replaced. We needed to carry a bottle of break fluid with us constantly; the only way to open the driver's side door from the inside was to wind down the window and put your arm through to the outside handle, and we were beginning to see the road pass beneath our feet, courtesy of a hole in the floor.

So I went looking for another car, second-hand of course, even though we could have afforded the best new car around. We had bought a new car once before (see Story 69) and didn't want to make the same mistake twice. It was my first experience of buying a car, as my father, and then my husband, had helped me on previous occasions. But I'd decided I'd look for myself this time — well, almost by myself: I had three young kids in tow.

Eventually I found a car I was interested in, after looking everywhere, and the salesman invited me, plus kids, into his office. I assumed he wanted to give me some more details about the vehicle so I sat down and parked the kids on the floor, each with something to eat to occupy them. The eldest two had bananas and the youngest a rusk.

The salesman dragged out his lap-top computer, placed it on the desk and proceeded to type away while asking me a series of questions: Name? Address? Phone number? Preferred insurance company?

By this time my kids were trying to smother his carpet with their mushy banana and soggy rusk. So naturally I was a little distracted, giving him answers blindly until he started with some more pertinent questions: Husband's employer? Wages? Other income?

"Hang on a minute!" I said. "What's this to do with this car?"

"I'm using this software to work out your finance costs," he replied.

"But I'm paying cash." And then it all twigged, but he continued:

"But I can show you how easy it is to finance this car for you. This software tells me it will cost you just $85 a week. How's that sound?"

"I can buy a house for less than that," I said, trying not to sound too smart. "I really just wanted to know more about the car. You know, how old? Previous owner? Log books? That sort of thing."

"Then you'll have to wait a few minutes for Bernie to return. He's the car expert. Most of us here just look after finance."

Author's note:

It's easy to understand how young kids get caught. Most of them think they are buying a car, when they are really buying finance. And when it sounds so cheap and easy, the consumer debt merry-go-round begins.

27. The furniture

It was late 1987 and we were out driving with an agent looking for property when she received a call on her two-way radio (remember those days before mobile phones?). The caller said that if the Woodwood Street property wasn't sold that day, then the owners, who had already been served with an eviction notice, would need to leave by the weekend — and it was already 3 p.m. Thursday.

The agent explained that she was familiar with the property and that the owners were twelve months behind in their payments to a building society, which was now taking legal action to recover the debt that had blown out from $40,000 to $48,000. (This was when the average cost of a house in that suburb was around $55,000.)

We weren't interested in houses in that particular area. We were looking for something with water frontage. But the agent insisted we take a quick look at the property, just in case. Within the hour we had negotiated a price of $50,000 with a thirty day contract, which gave the occupants 29 more days to move and more money than if the property had been take over as a "mortgagee in possession". It seemed to me that the owners would at least clear the $48,000 debt once the agent's commission had been paid.

But during the course of the conveyancing, it was discovered that a caveat had been placed on the title deed by a large finance company.

(A caveat on a title simply means that there is another party with a financial interest in the property, and it can't be sold until this third party is satisfied that either their money will be returned or the payments will be renegotiated. In fact it is a tactic used by many financial institutions to save on costly conventional mortgage documentation.)

On further investigation we found that the vendors of the property had borrowed $20,000 as a personal loan through the finance company to buy their furniture and electrical goods.

When we'd inspected the property prior to signing the contract, I had particularly noted that the furniture in the house was of high quality. The lounge was real leather, the sideboards fully timber with lead-light glass panels, the bed was king-size and there was a two-door ice-making fridge parked in the entrance way, too big for the space allotted in the kitchen.

There was no doubt it was truly expensive furniture — the kind I had always wanted but had decided could wait till later. I can tell you, it was not hard to see where the $20,000 had been spent, and ten years ago, that was a lot of money.

When I realised the situation, I felt I should try to help the couple who were being forced to sell their property. I was prepared to back off from the sale if they wanted the opportunity to sell their luxury furniture and pay restitution to the building society of the overdue amount of $8,000, thereby avoiding the necessity to sell their home at all.

Even if the furniture had been sold at half price for $10,000 it would have been enough to keep up the payments to both the building society and the finance company and allow them to retain their house. But to my utter amazement the woman explained:

"But I won't survive without my nice furniture. And even if I sell it, I'll still be in debt. So I may as well have something to show for all my hard work over the years."

I shook my head in disbelief. What would she have left to show for all her hard work after another ten years, I asked myself. So I reiterated that I was prepared to forgo the sale and tear up the contract if they wanted to take the opportunity to sell their furniture and save their house. But she just shook her head in loathing at the mere thought of selling any of her nice things, especially at a loss. And she restated her position:

"I'm sorry, I just can't. I've dreamed of this kind of furniture all my life and I'm not letting it go now."

As a last resort I offered them the chance to rent back the house so they wouldn't have to move. But as I found out later, by the time they had negotiated with the finance company to restructure the payments on their personal loan to an affordable level, they could only afford to rent a flat at about $80 per week. They simply couldn't afford to stay and rent their own house — even if we had discounted the rent by $20 to $130 per week, which we were willing to do as a gesture of goodwill.

On the day of settlement we drove out to the property to check that its condition had remained unchanged, and found the owners busy with a large removal van taking away their furniture. They definitely didn't have the kind of household items you could throw on the back of a hire trailer and shift yourself.

I chatted to the woman as the van was loaded up. She thanked me for giving them the extra 29 days to move and told me how happy she was that they could keep their furniture. I kept my mouth shut.

Author's note:

Defaults on housing loans are usually not the result of people having trouble keeping up with payments on them. They are usually caused by people having trouble keeping up with payments on both their housing loan *and* consumer type debt. Remember our lounge in Story 21? Having our $80 lounge instead of furniture like this woman's enabled us to buy her property — and many other properties as well.

28. The DINKS

Sara and Allan married in 1992 when they were in their early thirties. In the twelve years before, they both had well-paying jobs in Sydney, Sara as an executive's personal assistant and Allan as a tax accountant with a large company. When they married, however, they had no recognisable assets to their names, owning, rather, two upmarket cars, two wardrobes of designer clothes, costly jewellery, and countless CDs.

Following their marriage, they decided to buy a house, but realising that Sydney prices were well out of their reach they moved to Melbourne, where they could afford a more modern house for much less. They scraped together the minimum 5% deposit of $7,500 on a $150,000 property and settled in to their new way of life.

With both of them again obtaining well paid jobs in Melbourne, and with no children as yet, their monthly loan payments were comfortable. But having lived the good life for so long, they found it very difficult to adjust. They had always rented luxury apartments, bought nice clothes and dined at classy restaurants. Finally, Sara decided they had to cut back on visits to restaurants as eating out was eating up their budget. They could entertain their friends at home, she reasoned, but would need some better furniture for this plan.

So in 1995 they took out a personal loan for $10,000 to buy a new dining suite and matching lounge. As it was a personal loan, the bank didn't require security in the way of equity in their house, which they didn't have anyway. At first the extra payments were easy, and they enjoyed entertaining their friends at home.

However, it wasn't long before Sara and Allan found that, with a busy lifestyle and both still working, it was simply more convenient to dine out. This began putting a strain on their finances and after a year of struggling with both loans, and with their credit cards now at their limits, there were things they just couldn't afford to buy. According to Sara, she now "badly" needed new clothes to maintain her "executive" image at work, and Allan needed to update and add to his specialist CD collection.

They had heard it was possible to reduce overall loan payments by consolidating loans. So they went to their bank, where the lending officer told them they could consolidate their three loans, which now stood at $140,000 for their housing loan, $8,000 for their personal loan and $4,000 on credit cards, provided their house valued up to at least $160,000, which fortunately, or as you will soon see, unfortunately, it did.

The three loans were consolidated into one single principal and interest loan, reducing the monthly payments from $1,500 to $1,100. And the lending officer volunteered some friendly advice. If they continued making the original monthly payment of $1,500, the term of the loan would be reduced from 25 to 13 years, saving them a huge sum in interest.

However, Sara's view was that this would give them an extra $400 per month to spend on how they lived, and so she began to buy more clothes and Allan continued adding to his CD collection.

In 1997, with both Sara and Allan enjoying an increase in wages, they approached their local bank again.

"Now I can afford to borrow more," Sara told the lending officer as they requested another personal loan for $30,000 to buy a new-model car, and within the week the deed was done, the new car bought.

The story does not end there, however. When I spoke to Sara and Allan after a seminar in Melbourne recently, they had just begun to come to their senses. They were looking to the future and were thinking about buying an investment property and starting a family. Their question was how they could afford to do both, as their bank had not been very helpful.

The problem was that when they tried to again consolidate their loans and reduce their monthly payments so they could afford an investment property, they found it wasn't possible. The car loan had to stay as a personal loan, otherwise they would have negative equity, with their debts exceeding the value of their home. And a revaluation was not likely to show any substantial increase in the preceding twelve months.

But as well as not being able to afford an investment property, Sara couldn't afford to stop work to have a family. They realise now that in the last 20 years they have frittered away almost $2,000,000 of wages (in today's dollars) and have nothing to show for all that hard work except a smart car, designer clothes, furniture, CDs....

Author's note:

Sara and Allan are typical of what can happen when young DINKS (Double Income No Kids) spend beyond their means — and no bank could possibly have helped them. There was also no way I could pull a bunny out of the hat and show them how they could afford an investment property *and* start a family, or even do either, for that matter. Their negative equity was brought about by their own lavish lifestyle financed by consumer debt, something only they could fix. Sadly, they now realise it is up to them.

Sometimes there are grim tales in the media of people who have found themselves with negative equity in their homes, scaring many investors away from property investment for fear of falling into the same trap. The truth is that negative equity applies mostly to owner occupiers who have used every ounce of equity to finance consumer debt. Investors who have used every ounce of equity to borrow for appreciating property have no need to worry.

29. The food bill

I was about to enter a hotel lift following a seminar in Sydney last year when I was approached by a well dressed woman probably in her forties, who asked if I would mind answering just one question for her.

"We've thought about property investment before but we never seem to have any spare income. We can barely afford to buy food, so I don't see how I can afford to buy property too. I was hoping you could help me."

I was curious as to why such an obviously well-to-do woman would find herself in such an awful predicament. So I stepped back out of the lift and told her that although I didn't do private consultations, I might be able to give her a few pointers. Zoe welcomed the chance to describe her situation. Now, I know you are going to find this story unbelievable. I even thought, initially, she must be having me on. But this is what I heard:

"We live in a $500,000 home on Sydney's North Shore and between my husband and I, our annual income is $200,000. We have a mortgage of $300,000 and we lease two cars, a BMW and a four wheel drive.

"I also have three children at a private school costing $35,000 a year and we have a yearly family skiing holiday; and there's also a personal loan we have for our new kitchen. And that's about it."

I asked her for more information on her income and expenses and then, sadly, I saw she was not joking, but deadly serious. This is the rough table I drew up for her:

Income	**$200,000**
Expenses	
Tax	$80,000
House Payments	$30,000
Car Payments	$30,000
School Fees	$35,000
Annual Holiday	$10,000
Personal Loan Payments	$10,000
Left over for Living Expenses	**$5,000**

"Now you see what I mean," she said, as if to prove she was right in saying they had nothing left over for food, let alone money to buy an investment property, even if it would only cost $35 per week as I had just explained in the seminar.

I wasn't sure what to say. I re-checked the figures. Yes, she *was* right about not having enough money left over for even the food on the table, and I could see by the way she dressed, the $5,000 that was left over for living expenses would barely have covered her clothes and shoes.

So I told her that if she was serious about investing, both she and her husband would need to make a priority list of expenses.

"At the top, put the essentials such as tax, house payments and real living expenses for food, etc., then add in an amount to be invested. And follow this with the non-essential items such as car leases and holiday in order of preference and priority." I then explained to her:

"The bottom line is that if you really want to invest, something will need to drop off the bottom of the list."

It was quite clear to me what had gone wrong with their budget and what should be dropped off the bottom of the list. They had undertaken too much debt of the wrong kind, consumer debt, and by trading down one or both cars they could easily have bought two investment properties and still have everything else — kids at a private school and even the annual skiing holiday. But I wasn't about to dictate to her and her husband how to live their lives. So I told her again, trying to clarify the situation, how she could make this choice:

"It's just a case of prioritising, of modifying or eliminating your non-essential expenses so that there is enough left over for your investments. You have to think about what you really do need. Go over it with your husband and talk to him about your priorities."

"Many thanks," she said, "I'll think about it." So I left Zoe to think.

Author's note:

I warned you, the story was unbelievable. If I hadn't heard so many like it before, I would have had trouble believing it myself.

But it was all too true. Extravagant lifestyles financed by the wrong kind of debt — consumer debt — are usually responsible for this kind of predicament. *Remember Murphy's Second Law in Story 25?*

Your earnings will always equal your expenses.

This applies to high income earners, just as much as to low earners. Everyone has to set spending priorities, and investments have to come near the top of the list, not the bottom.

But this setting of priorities was not the answer that Zoe wanted to hear, for she would have to make some serious lifestyle changes. And therein is the problem. Lifestyles can be addictive — once you start, it is difficult to change.

30.   The miner

Several years ago I was invited by a mining company to present a talk to their workers. It was part of a regular program of talks organised by the social committee, to be entertaining or informative.

On this occasion, the topic was the advantages of buying an investment property prior to buying your own home. Since most of the miners lived in either rent free or heavily subsidised accommodation, the committee reasoned that this topic would be more than appropriate.

In essence, using an example I demonstrated how it was possible to borrow to buy a $150,000 property using a minimum deposit of $15,000. Assuming an interest bill of $10,000 per year (based on a $135,000 loan at 8%), I showed them step by step how it would be paid for with rent of $6,000 net annually and an annual tax refund of $4,000.

In other words, this property was neutrally geared and apart from the initial deposit of $15,000, it wasn't going to cost a cent from then on. I also suggested that in this special case it would be wise to take a principal and interest loan because even though the tax advantages would be lost over the years, it was important to build up an equity base from which to go on to buy more property.

The presentation was well received, judging by the many questions afterwards. Most questions were the familiar ones about the Capital Gains Tax, the 221D form (which enables PAYE tax instalments to be reduced), and depreciation on fixtures and fittings.

But when it was finished and I was about to leave the hall a young man spoke to me. He wanted to raise something he felt had not been covered. Sean proceeded:

"I came along here tonight because the info in the brochure we were given at work talked about tax advantages. But from your figures, I see that if I buy an investment property, I'll only get an initial tax refund of about $4,000. And if I keep paying off this loan, I'll get an even smaller tax refund in future.

"My problem is I'm currently paying nearly $40,000 a year in tax. So a tax refund of only $4,000 is like a drop in the ocean. It seems such a waste to keep on paying so much in tax. But buying and gearing an investment property doesn't seem to solve my tax problem."

"Yes," I agreed, "but the tax advantages are just a minor consideration. You should be looking at the investment as a whole."

"But what if I can invest in something that can save me $30,000 in tax in the first year alone."

So I asked him to give me more details about this investment.

"I have a good friend who wants to set up a business. He has a large acreage up here full of dams and he wants to stock them with freshwater yabbies. There's a really good market for them overseas, but he needs a lot of capital to build sheds for a covered nursery area and a processing plant.

"He says his accountant told him that if he sets up a syndicate of people, each borrowing $100,000 to put in, this accountant can structure it so we can claim all the losses upfront and get a tax refund of more than $30,000 in the first year alone, and then more in the following years.

"I think this sounds much better than your way of saving just $4,000 tax in one year and then even less after that. At that rate I'd probably save less than $10,000 in three years. This yabby idea seems a much better way of saving tax. What do you think?"

"Well of course it's a better way of paying less tax. But you have to look at what you're going to get out of this investment in the end. Is there any history of this type of yabby farming being successful here?"

"No, but that's why we think we'll make a killing on this venture. No one's ever done it in this area before."

"Perhaps there's a good reason why no one has ever done it before. Maybe it's just not a goer and other people have already worked that out. Personally, I don't invest in anything that eats. Have your friend and his accountant given you some idea of the risks involved?"

"Well, sort of. But he's a good friend and he wouldn't let me down."

"The only advice I can give is to sort out the difference between your friend's good intentions and your own good investments. I'd also warn you to be careful about borrowing money for the wrong reasons. You may well gain a lot in tax advantages initially, but in the end you could be left with nothing of value and a bad debt of $100,000. So think about why you are borrowing money in the first place. To save tax, or to invest?"

Author's note:

I have come across many cases where someone who is earning good wages borrows money to invest in a highly risky venture purely to save on tax. Unfortunately, these people often confuse saving money with saving on tax and forget about the original reason for investing.

The fact that Sean had worked in the mines for more than ten years earning an average of $100,000 per year, and yet had not saved one dollar in that time, in itself told me that he did not have a savings psyche.

By all means, borrow money to invest in something such as property where the risk of losing your capital is negligible, but don't borrow to invest purely for the tax savings, especially when the risk of losing your capital is very high.

7
Credit lines

At the risk of overloading an old cliche, I firmly believe:

Credit lines are the best thing since deregulation — and sliced bread.

They are wonderful tools of the financial industry — provided they are used correctly. Originally used by businesses as an overdraft, they are in essence a pre-approved loan secured by a mortgage over property, usually residential, and provide credit to a preset limit at reasonable interest rates.

Today they are not only used by businesses as cheap overdrafts, but by home owners and investors. Indeed, they can now be used to borrow for anything at all — and here is the problem.

The good news is that credit lines are great when used in relation to investment opportunities such as renovations or the acquisition of more property. They offer on-tap finance at reasonable rates, less than for a personal unsecured loan, and allow access to money already repaid into a loan. In effect, they make property a liquid investment; like having cash in the bank.

The bad news is that there's a great temptation to use them as an open purse with money available for anything that takes one's fancy. When used this way, they function as an oversized credit card, with the added danger that the large increase in debt from the purchase of consumer goods can greatly decrease net worth and, ultimately, cause poverty in retirement.

But credit lines, as I said at the beginning, can be wonderful tools, and the following stories about people who have used them should help you distinguish between their good and bad uses.

31. The magic wand

Zac and Ali are like most young couples with a home loan — they knew they should pay it off as soon as they could. They bought their first home in 1991 with a loan of $110,000 and settled down to make the monthly repayments. Ali continues:

"We knew we should get rid of our home loan, but it was so hard paying any more than the required monthly amount. We were prepared to try anything, even switching to fortnightly payments. But the loan still didn't seem to disappear quickly enough.

"Then we were approached by someone in a shopping centre who was marketing a new style of loan which sounded interesting. He told us that if we converted our home loan to a credit line, this would help us pay out our loan quickly. He explained that money sitting in the account would reduce the term of the loan by cutting back the interest. So we decided to give it a go. But after three years, we seemed to be no better off. We'd thought we would make a big hole in the loan but it was just a little dent. That's why I phoned you. We would like to invest in more property but we just don't seem to be able to reduce this home loan."

So I explained to Ali how best to tackle her problem.

"Fortnightly payments and credit lines help, but the *only* way to pay off a loan more quickly is to put more money into it."

Author's note:

There's simply no magic way to pay off a home loan more quickly. Fortnightly payments, where you make 26 half payments instead of 12 full payments per year, can help by effectively adding an extra full payment per year. This can take a few years off the term of a loan.

And a credit line also helps by reducing the amount of interest accruing. However, if you believe that a credit line is a magic wand for paying off home loans quick, you're in for a shock. The fact that money sits in the account saving on interest certainly helps. But it will only reduce the term of the loan by a few years, not 10 years as you might hope for.

The trick in using a credit line to pay off your home loan faster is to put all your wages and spare money into it and then withdraw the absolute minimum, giving you a net payment of much more than the basic regular payment. It is those extra amounts left in permanently that will reduce the home loan quickly, not the extra amounts left in short term.

Of course, there is the reverse psychology that the mere act of making a withdrawal makes you think more about it so you don't withdraw as often, but no matter what the logic, there's no getting around the fact that bigger payments and smaller withdrawals are the answer to home loan reduction.

32. Building the loan

I met Shane and Gina late last year. They had a significant loan on their home but were keen to get started buying investment property. Twenty years ago they'd had no home loan and were in a great position to buy more property — but didn't. Gina tells her story:

"After saving a deposit of $8,000, we bought our first home in 1974 for $25,000. We both worked really hard to pay off the $17,000 mortgage, and we did in about five years.

"The problem was that after the hard slog, we sat back to start a family and enjoy ourselves, believing we had accomplished all there was to do. So the next fifteen years just slipped away. With no rent or mortgage to pay, and with Shane earning good money, we just kept spending on things we never had before — nice furniture and clothes and dining out.

"In 1994, we decided to buy a new car. The bank manager set up a new type of loan called a credit line for $50,000 against the value of our house, which by then was worth $120,000. With $40,000 we bought our four wheel drive, and had $10,000 to spare. The bank manager suggested we use the extra credit to start an investment plan. Did we want to talk to a financial planner? No, we're only forty, we thought. Plenty of time.

"Within a year we had spent the extra $10,000 on things for the house. The credit line worked so well that we went back three times to extend it. We took the kids overseas, put in a swimming pool, and then we bought a car for our daughter. Each time, the bank manager suggested we talk to a financial planner, and each time I told him we would do it later.

"Anyway, when we enquired about a loan for a boat, the bank had our house valued and we were told we didn't have enough equity. Our house was worth $130,000 but our loan had built up to $110,000. And to think that twenty years ago we had it all paid off. Somehow we had used up all our capital and all we had to show for it was a not-so-new car, some travel momentos, and a pool that the kids no longer used. We realised that the bank manager had been telling us things we weren't listening to. We should have been building net worth, not simply rebuilding the loan.

"But things are going to change. We've set ourselves a ten year plan to get rid of this home loan — again — and we're going to use this same line of credit to buy an investment property."

Author's note:

One year later, Shane and Gina have reduced the debt on their credit line enough to allow them to borrow for a deposit for their first investment property, something they now know they could have done twenty years ago had they not used their equity to borrow to buy consumer goods.

33. The family farm

This story at first glance might seem like a gross contradiction of the previous story. Having told you not to use a credit line to borrow to buy consumer items, I am going to tell you about Byron, who uses a credit line to do exactly that — to borrow for his living expenses. But with Byron it is very different — he is a classic case of asset rich, income poor.

He lives on 10 acres of absolute waterfront land that has been in his family for forty years. But now that he has retired from farming due to a serious back injury, he has no income. Byron is reluctant to sell the land just now because the whole area is in the process of being re-zoned from rural farming to medium and high density residential.

If he sells now he might get $500,000, but if he waits for another few years, he considers the land could be worth more than $2,000,000. This is because similar properties in the area that have been re-zoned have recently sold for this. And he can't even sell a "bit" of his land now, because the minimum lot size for farming in the area is 10 acres.

Byron explained the problem to his local bank manager who could see the potential of the land, and suggested he set up a credit line for Byron for $100,000. Byron figured that he and his wife could get by on $20,000 per year for the next two or three years, knowing they could live well when the land was eventually re-zoned. And even if the entire loan were to be used up with capitalised interest and draw-downs, he figured he'd be much better off in three years by eating into his capital now rather than selling.

And so Byron went ahead and set up the credit line, which he now uses for normal everyday living expenses.

Author's note:

Byron's position of being asset rich, income poor is very common, particularly among elderly people who have no income apart from an age pension, but who own their own home. Whilst, generally speaking, I wouldn't suggest using a credit line to spend on living expenses, there are exceptions to the rule. Byron's case was one.

As an interesting aside, one of the many new financial products now available is being offered by the Bank of Scotland in the United Kingdom. They are offering a credit line with an interest rate of 0%. An article in the London *Times* on November 10, 1996 described the loan:

> ...   the Shared Appreciation Mortgage could be the bedrock of financial planning for the millions of people who need to release equity. It works by allowing borrowers to borrow up to 25% of the value of their home. On sale or death, three times the loan will be taken from the growth in the property's value.

34. The cash contract

Bill and Penny were all set to buy their first investment property and were negotiating on the asking price of $150,000. They offered $140,000 with a two weeks "subject to finance" clause in the contract, but the vendors wouldn't budge below $148,000.

The agent explained to Bill and Penny that the vendors urgently wanted to move during the June school holidays, so a "subject to finance" clause in the contract would make them very nervous: there was no way they would accept a lower offer with any uncertainty about it. But, according to the agent, they would readily accept a lower price for a cash contract, maybe even $140,000, as this would ensure they could move on time.

Bill and Penny told the agent they intended using their principal place of residence valued at $450,000 to finance the deal and that the property they were buying would not be mortgaged. But the agent responded:

"A finance clause is a finance clause no matter how you borrow it."

Bill and Penny told him they had no hope of rounding up the cash, so they would have to stick with the finance clause. The vendors refused to sign the contract they submitted and one day later accepted an unconditional cash contract from someone else for $140,000.

Quite let down by missing out, Bill and Penny consulted their bank about a pre-approved loan. They figured that if they could show a letter of finance approval to a vendor, they might have a chance of getting a good deal on a property. But they found they could do better than a pre-approved loan: the bank could give them a line of credit allowing them to pay cash for any property they might want to buy in the future.

"Cash is cash, even if you borrow it," the bank manager said.

Bill and Penny had sufficient collateral in their $450,000 home to set up a credit line for $350,000, enough for them to "pay cash" for at least two investment properties. They now buy all their properties with a cash contract, although, as Bill says, they often add a building inspection clause as a cover, because it doesn't seem as off-putting as a finance clause.

Author's note:

Credit lines are great for purchasing properties for "cash". But they can also be used to mix and match loans. One option might be to draw down a deposit for a property from a credit line, and then obtain additional monies from a completely different financial institution. Another option might be to use the credit line to buy a property in a hurry, after which you can take as much time as you like to arrange fixed-interest finance from a different source. The sky's the limit once you start to think laterally about how to use a credit line to buy investment property.

35. Cash in the bank

Ossie has six investment properties. He also is very cautious about covering himself for all the things that can possibly go wrong. To this end, he has always ensured he has $10,000 put aside in the bank for each property he has bought. So by the time he came to talk to me at the end of a seminar, Ossie had more than $60,000 sitting in an account.

"It seems such a waste," he said. "All this money sitting there and the interest rate at the moment is a pittance at 2%. And I can't put it in a term deposit to get more interest because it will be tied up and I wouldn't be able to get it unless I cried poor and lost some interest as well."

I could understand his problem. In my book *Building Wealth through Investment Property* I advocated the use of cash reserves as a means of "financial insurance" and suggested:

> ....   cash to the value of at least 5% of your total loans should be set aside for ... unscheduled expenses (even if this money is borrowed with your loan). There's nothing like money in the bank to help you sleep better. Your ability to get your hands on money immediately can alleviate ... temporary crises — maybe you can't do overtime this month, or your property may become vacant the same week you have to pay school fees.

At the same time I suggested the use of a "cheque-book mortgage", which was the forerunner of today's line of credit. However, these types of loans were originally limiting because they often required a mortgage over an entire property. They were also not freely available (sometimes only to people of high net worth) and often costly to set up. But that was 1992.

Six years later the credit line has become very popular and is much more readily available — and very cost effective. It is possible even to squeeze a credit line as a second mortgage on top of another loan, so that the entire property is not usurped with just one credit line. The point is, credit lines have become commonplace in the financial industry.

So I suggested to Ossie that if he established a credit line against one of his properties he would have access to his money quickly, but only pay interest on the money he used. At the same time, he could reduce his cash reserves to whatever level he felt was comfortable.

"A credit line is better than cash in the bank," I explained to him.

Author's note:

If you're planning to use a credit line in lieu of cash in the bank, or as well as, make sure it is set up in good time before you need it. It's funny how banks love to give you money when you don't need it, but never want to give you any when you do (see Story 87).

8
The right time

We all accept that such a thing as a property cycle exists. Most of us have seen at least one cycle, some of us two, and a few of us six or seven. The typical cycle involves rising interest rates, stagnating property values followed by falling interest rates, and rising property values, the whole cycle lasting about seven years, more or less.

Does this mean we sit back and wait to buy property at that point when property values are just beginning to climb rapidly? Absolutely not! As I pointed out in my book, *Building Wealth through Investment Property*:

For short-term property investors, the timing of these cycles is most important, but for long-term investors, these fluctuations even out.

I have never used cycles as an indicator of when to buy investment property. We can all look back and pinpoint the precise times when it may have been economically best to have bought property. But hindsight only makes us wiser, not wealthier.

My philosophy was, is, and always will be, to buy property at any time I can afford to and hang on for the long term. In other words, waiting for the right time to buy property is not nearly as important as keeping for a long time. Or in case you missed the point, time, not timing is the key.

The following stories are about people who bought property regardless of the time, and people who watched and waited for the right time to jump on the band wagon. But as I once heard:

"By the time you identify a band wagon, it's usually gone."

36. The real estate guru

Fred Johnson is a real estate guru I have respected for many years. He has been investing in residential property for more than 45 years, since he bought his first property in 1954 with a deposit of just £120 ($240), the only time he ever injected capital. Fred has written many time-honoured books on property, including *How to get Real Estate Rich* (1969), and a recent one, with his son Brett, called *The Wealth Power of Property*, in which he expounds his views on timing:

> Consistently throughout the past 45 years, people have been telling me that it's not a good time to invest in property. In the early 50s when a home loan was as rare as hens' teeth, they said — it's not a good time to buy; there is no money available; prices will not rise. In the late 50s when exports were flagging, they said the economy was heading for disaster: don't buy property, interest rates were going up, import quotas were being cut and world prices for wool and wheat had dropped.

> The Menzies credit squeeze of 1961 was a good reason not to buy property. Drying up of credit; lack of confidence in the economy. The doom sayers said property as an investment was finished and would never return to its old glory. In the late 60s, Great Britain, our biggest export customer, was negotiating to join the EEC. Menzies raced to London to point out the error of their ways. He was unsuccessful and proclaimed that Great Britain's entry to the EEC would make previous recessions look like a boom. Don't invest in property now, they said.

> The early 70s saw low inflation. Property would not increase in value, they said. Then in the mid 70s, there was high inflation, high unemployment and then recession. The OPEC oil crisis of the late 70s caused the experts to say that property prices would drop as people and industry could not survive the expansion of our cities as oil prices soared. Property was out of fashion once again.

> The abolition of negative gearing in the mid 80s had people saying — don't buy property now, there's no tax advantages. In the early 90s we had another recession and low inflation with a flood of headlines such as "values cannot rise when inflation is low".

> Consistently for the past 45 years, experts have been telling me that the time is not right to invest in property. But what I observed in retrospect was that when everybody was telling me the time was wrong, it was right.

Author's note:

I wish I'd known about Fred Johnson thirty years ago.

37. The Greek immigrant

One of the lengthier letters I have received came from a proud Greek gentleman named Gus. It was hand written in somewhat broken English, but the message was clear. He always felt he was doing the right thing by his family in buying investment property but had little encouragement along the way. He happily related how his stubbornness won him through on the day:

Many times in the past 40 years, my family and friends tried to talk me into selling my properties. I always listened but I never sold.

My family came from Greece in 1952 and settled in Melbourne. I was nineteen and I hardly knew any English. My father bought a fruit shop which my mother and I and my two brothers worked in day and night.

One year later, I married a Greek girl, like all good Greek boys do, and we lived with my family at the back of the shop until I had saved up enough to buy a house. I bought my first property in 1955 for £2,000 ($4,000) — it was nothing fancy. Then after two years I bought the land next door.

With three children under five, my wife wanted me to sell the land in 1960 to help pay for the kids but I didn't. I told her that being young, the children wouldn't eat much. And then my grandfather came out from Greece and we built a house for him on the land I had bought that my wife wanted to sell and he rented it from us. With the extra rent, two years later I could then buy another property in the next street.

In 1965, with my three children at school, my grandfather who still lived next door told me I should sell the house I had bought in the next street to help pay for their schooling. But I thought I would be better to teach them the right way about money.

So I bought one more house in the same street. The kids didn't really need any extra money for their schooling — Pa just thought I should think of the kids first and I told him I was. How else would they learn about money?

Again in 1970 my wife wanted me to sell a property to pay for my daughter's wedding, but I thought I would be better to teach her and her husband the right way about money so I decided to buy another property and I bought a house in the same street again. I then had five properties, my own, my grandfather's and my three houses in the next street. I paid for my daughter's wedding with some of the extra money I borrowed for the last house.

In 1974 property prices almost doubled and I was glad I had bought all those properties. My wife was too. But by 1977 I thought I was going to go broke with the high interest rates because I had borrowed money for all these houses. My children wanted me to sell but I managed to hang on by making arrangements with my solicitor just to pay the interest. And then after thinking I might have to sell some property, I find I can buy one more. I was glad I did because in 1981 prices increased.

In 1986, my friends kept telling me to sell because I had already made a lot of money out of property, and there was no more to be made, they told me. Nothing has happened to property for five years, they said, so you should sell up and put your money into shares. No need to tell you what happened to shares the next year.

But my rents were very good so I didn't take any notice of them, thank God, and I could afford to buy three more properties. My wife thought I was bananas and my children thought I would lose all of their inheritance. Then in 1989 my properties all went up in value — once again. Everybody was happy.

In 1992, my friends told me to sell as nothing much would happen with low inflation, they said. I learned by now that when I hear the word sell, I buy. So I bought five more properties and my interest bill is now half what it was because rates have fallen.

My wife and children came up to me the other day and thanked me for not listening to them. I said I did listen, I just never took any notice.

Author's note:

Gus is a wise old gentleman who could have written my two earlier books forty years ago — and he told me so.

It never ceases to amaze me that there are people out there in the community who knew all these things long before I did. I often wonder why I never got to meet any of them when I was much younger and knew nothing about property. But as you will see in Story 57, I did meet one of them when I was young, I just didn't recognise it. They say that when the student is ready, the teacher appears. I was obviously not ready to learn at the time.

There is so much to be learned from these people who have been investing in property for a long time. One thing they all tell you is: if you wait for the right time to buy, you'll never buy anything at all. And if you sell when everyone says sell, you'll never have anything at all. The trick is to buy whenever you can afford to. In other words, buy when it suits you financially, not when it's economically correct.

38. The lucky couple

When Marlene told me her story at a Perth seminar in 1992, I thought it was an interesting example of how investors could turn adversity into opportunity. However, reading it after she wrote it down for me recently, I decided it was more about her friends!

Our friends all think we are lucky because we always seem to be in the right place at the right time. But we don't think so because we did a lot of things our friends could have done but didn't.

My husband has been a road worker with the local council since he left school 15 years ago, and I am a secretary for the same council. We accidentally bought our first home 12 years ago when we went with some friends to an auction looking for cheap furniture for the place we were renting. We were very late and by the time we got there, only the house was left to sell — the house, not the land.

No one else wanted to buy it, not even our friends because it needed a lot of work doing to it, so we bought it for $100 on a credit card. Our friends shook their heads in disbelief.

Then we had to find a block of land. There was nothing we could afford in the Perth area, so we settled for a block just south of Perth for $15,000. Our friends thought we were mad because the land was behind the sandhills in a swamp and we had to have it filled.

The bank wasn't impressed either and gave us the money as a personal loan at more than 17% interest because they reckoned the land wasn't worth anything and any mortgage would be a waste of time and money.

It cost us another $5,000, which we borrowed on credit card, to get the house moved down there and have it re-stumped. We decided on tall stumps because of the swampy ground, and then we found that we had a glimpse of the ocean, across the top of the sandhills.

We worked hard on the house for the next two years, but we had got tired of all the travelling backwards and forwards to the city and so we decided to sell and move in closer. Some real estate agents said they thought we'd get $120,000. We were flabbergasted when we did — a place the bank wouldn't mortgage! But the place did have water views now and there had been quite a bit of development in the area as well, which had bumped values along. All our friends said we were just lucky it worked out so well.

In 1986, with the $100,000 we had after paying out the personal loan (we had paid off the credit card earlier), we bought two more houses, for cash, for $50,000 each. We lived in one and rented the other. We had only been in the house for a month when Andy, my husband, wanted to buy some more property.

I had thought I'd leave work to have a family, so I wasn't keen. But Andy was sure that the rents would pay for the mortgage. He was good with sums. So we bought another house with a loan of $55,000. This time we went to a different bank.

Our friends thought we were mad for borrowing all that money when negative gearing had just been axed and we wouldn't get any tax advantages. Our family thought we were going in over our heads, just like they did when we bought our "swamp" house.

So when I left work after six months to start a family, everyone was convinced we were daft. I would have left sooner but it took me almost six months to really be confident that Andy was right about the rents covering the mortgage.

By the end of 1990 our properties had all doubled in value and our friends and family were saying:

'Geez you were lucky! You always seem to be in the right place at the right time!'

We don't think we were lucky. We just bought whatever we could, whenever we could afford to. We didn't have a crystal ball to see what was coming. We now own six properties in the Perth area and we know that if we had listened to our friends and family, we would still be renting today. Andy still works for the council and I have gone back part-time for two days a week.

When we look back over the properties we have bought, I think to myself that every time we did buy something, our friends could have done exactly the same as we did, but they didn't. They were at the auction and could have bought the house. They came with us when we bought the land in the swamp and could have bought the block next door. They could have bought their own home in 1986 when we bought our three properties in that one year.

Our friends are still renting and although we have encouraged them to at least try to buy their own home, they just say how lucky we were, and that it could never happen to them. I keep telling them it certainly won't happen to them if they do nothing.

Author's note:

I believe that we make our own luck. The harder we work, the luckier we get, so they say. So as I see it, Andy and Marlene's success had nothing to do with being in the right place at the right time. It was simply about doing something.

39. The sheet of paper

I have never been one to sit and watch the economic clock and wonder about the right time to buy property. The right time for us was determined first by our need, because of our nomadic lifestyle, and later by whether or not we could afford to. "When", as based on economic timing, was never a factor and never will be.

I well remember the day in late November, 1972, when Ian and I sat in a bank manager's office looking for our very first loan. Neither of us had ever borrowed money before. Not a car loan, not a personal loan, nothing. So it was a very daunting experience.

We went prepared with every piece of information I figured we would need. Savings passbook accounts, salary statements, University degrees, drivers' licences, and a few personal references from various sources that said no more than we were who we said we were.

The bank manager sat behind a large desk that seemed to span at least three metres. And I felt as though we were being quizzed by the highest ranking police officer in the land, having just been indicted for grand theft. How much was the property worth? How much had we saved? How long had we been working for? Were there any relatives who banked with this particular bank? What were our living expenses? How much money did we want to borrow?

To tell the truth, we didn't have a clue about how much money we needed to borrow. We didn't even know if we could afford a loan. We knew nothing about property, about investing, about borrowing money. We were young, aged 22, and had been engaged for just four weeks. We'd planned to get married in the December of that year, which was only a month away, and the only thing we were sure of was that we would like to start our life together in our own house, however humble that might be.

We knew we couldn't afford much, so the house we had put on contract was very basic. On a scale of one to ten it probably rated two. It was a high-set chamferboard, all of 7.4 squares, with three small bedrooms (two were too small even to fit in beds). The price was $12,500 and we'd been able to scratch up $4,000 (mostly because Ian had saved all his money for a few years while I had spent mine overseas).

"We think we'll need a loan of $9,000," we answered meekly.

When we left an hour later, I felt as though we had just been through a cyclone in a tin boat. But the worst part was the waiting afterwards. The not knowing if we qualified for the loan or not. There had been no glint in the bank manager's eye. No tell-tale body movements and definitely no verbal indication that the loan would go through.

Two weeks later we were informed that a loan for $8,900 had been approved. Back in those days, banks ruled the world, so I guessed they had to show a bit of one-upmanship in not lending us the full $9,000. And so we settled on our very first property.

Three years later we bought our second and then a few years later another and then another. Each was bought in the same way. We went to the bank, sat trembling in the manager's office while we answered a series of questions about our incomes and then went home to wait for the phone to ring to find out whether or not we had secured the loan.

Each property was bought out of necessity rather than as part of an investment strategy based on "now is the right time to buy". The first was bought because we were about to get married, the second because we had moved to the other side of town, the third because we thought we couldn't afford to buy in Sydney so we bought a property in Brisbane for when we returned, and the fourth because we needed a bigger place for our family.

We never knew ahead whether we qualified for a loan, had no concept of making a good investment decision, and at that stage, did not see ourselves as investing in property. Our motive for our purchases was personal need.

When we were about to buy our fifth property (which was the very start of our planned investment strategy), I realised — at last — that there was such a thing as "lending criteria" for banks. So for this loan, I decided to go prepared. Totally. I took a single sheet of paper.

I had spent the night before preparing this. I drew a line down the centre and on the left side at the top marked the heading "Income" and across on the right side wrote the heading "Expenses".

On the left, I listed our wages, rents and interest. On the right, I listed our tax liabilities, rental expenses, loan repayments and living expenses. Then I subtracted one from the other to give our net income.

Next, I listed our assets on the left, our liabilities on the right and subtracted one from the other to give our net worth. I gave this sheet to the bank manager and simply said:

"Here's a list of our incomes and expenses, and assets and liabilities. As you can see, our income is greater than our expenses and we have a substantial net worth. So we'd like a $53, 500 loan for another property."

It worked like a charm, and we got exactly the amount we had asked for, not $100 less.

I didn't in fact know what their lending criteria were, only that we wanted to buy more property (by now we were well and truly committed investors) and this was simply because we had worked out that we could afford another loan.

Nowadays, I prepare two such sheets, one for our current situation, and one for the new situation, assuming we get the loan. The table below should give you an idea of how you too can set out your information on one page.

Assets & Liabilities Statement

Income		Expenses	
Husband's Wages	$40,000	Husband's Tax	$2,000
Wife's Wages	$10,000	Wife's Tax	$1,000
Rental Income	$45,000	Rental Expenses	$10,000
Interest on Deposits	$1,000	Loan Repayments	$45,000
Other Income	$1,000	Living Expenses	$25,000
Total Income	**$97,000**	**Total Expenses**	**$83,000**
NET INCOME	**$14,000**		
Assets		Liabilities	
Principal Residence	$200,000	Loan A	$200,000
6 Smith St	$150,000	Loan B	$150,000
105 Brown St	$140,000	Loan C	$120,000
96 Black St	$180,000	Loan D	$25,000
15 White St	$220,000	Credit Card	$1,000
33 Rose St	$90,000		
Total Assets	**$980,000**	**Total Liabilities**	**$496,000**
NET WORTH	**$484,000**		

To this day, I have never sat back and waited for the right time to buy property. I still go to the bank manager (or rather, he comes to us now) with a sheet of paper with a line down the centre showing exactly how we can afford to borrow for more property.

40. The waiting game

Des and Bronwyn are a young couple in their twenties who decided to buy their own home almost immediately after they were married in 1989. Des had been teaching a year and had saved almost $14,000 from his salary of $25,000. Bronwyn had been a typist for four years earning an average of $15,000 per year. She had been on a trip overseas, but had still saved $8,000 in the two years since.

So they had $22,000 between them. The next step was to find a property, but they still had one more obstacle — the "helpful" friends and rellies.

"Don't buy a house now," they said. "You've missed the boat."

The type of house they had their eye on could have been bought for $50,000 a year before. It would now cost about $90,000. Brisbane, like most other cities, had just been through a property boom with price hikes of more than 60% in less than twelve months.

"Wait a few more years and buy *just* before the next boom," the couple were constantly told.

One very helpful friend (who owned no property) could even quote the complete history of property prices in Brisbane over the past thirty years. This was the right time to buy and that was the right time to sell and if they had bought one year ago they would have been thousands of dollars better off. He thought Des and Bronwyn should wait five years, and get in before the peak of the next seven year cycle.

But Des and Bronwyn were set on their goal. They didn't want to play the waiting game. So they bought an $80,000 house in outer suburban Brisbane ("way out" as Bronwyn described it) with a $20,000 deposit and a loan of $60,000.

When I talked to Des and Bronwyn in 1994, five years later, they owed only $10,000. They weren't too sure about the value of their property, but did know that even if it hadn't increased, their net worth was now at least $80,000. So while their friends were spending money and waiting for the next boat to arrive to take them to financial freedom, Des and Bronwyn were already on it.

Author's note:

At the time of writing, Des and Bronwyn are travelling in Europe, with a fully paid for house to come back to.

History makes us all property experts. The trick is to get into the market at any time, and hang on. Irrespective of the timing of property cycles, a home loan is a form of committed savings.

9
Mountains to molehills

We are lucky to have a wonderful ninety year old neighbour with a great perspective on life. This is a short poem he has written:

Make mountains into molehills,
Torrents into streams,
Deserts into pastures,
Real things. Not just dreams.

If only we all thought like he does. There are so many times in our lives when we are faced with seemingly insurmountable problems. The one thing I have found that helps us overcome these problems is to have a positive attitude to life. I know at times it's easier said than done.

......

Having just written that, as if to test me, I received a fax from one of our letting agents saying we had termites in one of our rental houses. She phoned a minute later to ask permission to organise treatment, expecting I'd be upset about the discovery of termites and the cost of the quote.

But I had already had time to digest the problem and gave it the green light. A mental flashback had quickly shown me that the house, worth about $130,000 on the present market, had cost us $23,500 in 1976. It has always been rented, with few vacancies, and has cost us very little in the 22 years.

The termite problem was minor, really, considering what the house had made us, not cost. I hope that the succeeding stories will help you to turn mountains into molehills, as in our neighbour's vision in his poem.

41.   The whingers

One of our property managers recently told me about a house he has been managing for a young couple named Pam and Dean. They own several properties and always insist they be contacted immediately about maintenance problems. This particular property they have owned for more than five years and it has had the same tenants since day one. The tenants have looked after the property and it has always looked immaculate.

In being so fastidious, however, the tenants have always found faults with the place, with Pam and Dean often receiving calls from the agent saying "Mr and Mrs S... want something fixed". Cracks in the brickwork, leaking gutters, chipped roof tiles, worn carpet, poor TV reception, cold hot water, sagging clothes line, split ceiling plaster, leaking shower, torn curtains, broken hinges on the oven door and a falling-down fence are just some of the complaints over the five years.

The agent explained that it was just as well that Pam and Dean were experienced property investors, and were able to put these problems in perspective. Anyone else would be thinking they had bought the worst house in the world. Or been put off rental property altogether.

In fact, the couple knew this house was sound as they had bought it half finished: the first half had been built by a craftsman boat builder and they themselves had employed the best tradesmen to finish it off.

So when the managing agent's first maintenance report indicated that the falling-down fence was no more than a loose paling that took two minutes to fix, and the leaking shower was a split washer that took even less time to change, they figured that the tenants were just a little prone to exaggeration and if it was really that bad, they would have moved out long before now.

One night recently, the agent rang Pam and Dean. The tenants had an enquiry. The husband had received a job promotion, the wife had been left some money from an aunt and so they now were in a position to buy a property. Good, thought Pam out loud, they must be moving out. But no. And the agent quoted verbatim what the tenants had said:

"We've looked at a lot of property since deciding to buy a house for ourselves, and we like this one so much we'd like to buy it."

Author's note:

Whingeing tenants sometimes put people off becoming property investors. That's where good property managers are useful — they sort out serious problems from trivial complaints. But "problem" tenants like these are often good to have. You can be sure that the property is being well looked after. You just have to put the "problems" in perspective.

42.   The perfect house

Having just finished paying off the loan on their home, Jill and Peter decided to buy an investment property. They had been very finicky with the renovations to their own house, sometimes spending weeks looking for the right door knob and so on.

This particular house was their sixth in less than ten years. Each time they'd bought, they'd got half way through renovating, then decided there was something they didn't quite like about the house, consequently selling it before the renovations were completed.

Their obsession carried over to their choice of investment property. They spent six months looking for the perfect house and finally found *the* one. Every night and every weekend for the next month they worked on it until finally the house was ready for renting.

Two months later, the managing estate agent advised them there was a blockage in the sewer. He had called in a plumber who'd discovered that the roots of a fig tree had invaded the old clay pipe which would need to be replaced with PVC. In the plumber's opinion, it was not a large job. But it was too much for Jill and Peter. They decided to sell the house, which they did for no profit, and look for a trouble-free one.

They soon found another place and again set about making it perfect before renting it out. Six months later, following a hail storm, the agent rang to say the pointing in the roof ridge had cracked and the roof was leaking. Although covered by insurance, they decided to sell, barely recouping their costs.

Not to be beaten, believing the perfect house was somewhere, if they could find it, Jill and Peter spent another three months searching, and on finding what they were looking for, began the usual renovations.

Some twelve months later, the agent sent them a routine inspection report. The tenants were looking after the property well, but two internal doors needed trimming as a result of house movement caused by the dry weather. Most houses have similar settling problems, the agent wrote at the bottom of the report, so not to worry. Jill and Peter didn't worry, they sold the house.

Author's note:

This happened almost 10 years ago and every one of those properties Jill and Peter bought has more than doubled in value. The perfect house is like the perfect child — it doesn't exist. Most buildings have a few minor problems from time to time, but they must be put into the context of what we are trying to achieve by investing in property: not so much a perfect property, as a financially independent retirement.

43. The landlord

In 1996, I attended a talk organised by the Rental Tenancy Authority. The new rules associated with tenants' bonds (as they related to Queensland properties) were explained to a large audience of real estate agents, landlords and tenants.

There was a question time at the end, which one man in the audience dominated by a rapid-fire series of questions:

"What is the RTA going to do about the time lapse between when I can legally evict a tenant and when I need to? I have had instances where I need to immediately evict a drunken tenant for the safety of other tenants in the building, but my hands are tied.

"When will the RTA sidestep the Small Claims Tribunal if there is a dispute? It costs me $50 every time I go — which can be once a week.

"Why is there a law now that lets tenants organise maintenance work that I am then forced to pay for?

"Why can't I keep furniture left behind by tenants in lieu of rent?

"Why can't I charge rent up to two months in advance so that the rent covers the time it takes to get an eviction order?"

And so on. The chairman was adept and very patient in responding, but I was beginning to think everyone who was present (except tenants) would have the impression that every tenant in every property caused serious problems. So I decided to ask a few pertinent questions to help put things in perspective.

I asked the chairman if he could tell us how many tenancies resulted in serious disputes. His answer was that, of the 200,000 bonds lodged with the RTA annually, less than 1% went before the Small Claims Tribunal! In other words, that particular investor had painted a very distorted picture of what happens during a normal tenancy.

Author's note:

Problem tenants do exist, but this has to be viewed in perspective. Few cause major problems and those who do are usually in properties that are not up to par. I found out later through an agent who'd also attended the session that the disgruntled investor owned 50 bedsits and no agent was willing to manage them. The bedsits were all dilapidated and in two buildings worth almost $1,000,000, so each was worth about $20,000. Do you get the picture?

This landlord had self-inflicted tenancy problems because of the dismal types of property he was letting and the types of tenant behaviour they either attracted or encouraged. Good properties usually attract good tenants.

44. Sleeping on it

Ron and Julie married at the end of 1996, immediately after they'd graduated as physiotherapists. They rented a unit and within six months had saved $10,000 from their wages as physios at the same large hospital and decided it was time to buy a property.

They were keen on the idea of buying a lot of property and wanted to get started as soon as they could. And although they would have liked to have bought their own home immediately, they realised they were much better off to buy an investment property first.

Where they were renting was perfect for the time being as it was very close to their work (just a short walk to Ron's work and just a short bus ride to Julie's) and with no children, they didn't need a big backyard. Also, they both had very good incomes. And they figured that if they could save on tax by buying a negatively geared investment property instead of their own home, they could put both the tax saving and the rent towards the loan, and pay it off even more quickly.

As they had no intention of ever living in this property, the precise location was not critical. So they looked far and wide for something suitable. After weeks of inspections, they found what they were looking for in the outer western suburbs of Sydney.

The asking price for the property was $130,000, but Ron and Julie had set themselves a limit of $120,000. And the best deal they could negotiate was $125,000, the vendors not budging because they needed every single dollar for the new house they were building around the corner.

So Ron and Julie went away to sleep on the problem and the next day went back to the agent with an offer. The deal was that the vendors could rent their own house back for six months while they were building if they would accept an offer of $120,000. And the offer was accepted.

Ron and Julie were very pleased with themselves. In fact, they went out to celebrate how smart they had been in negotiating a deal on their very first investment property. But their smugness was short-lived. The next day, they eagerly went to their bank to try to organise a loan for their property, but struck another snag — a big one. Their loan application was refused point blank.

As the bank manager explained it, their problem was not their $70,000 in combined wages. They had ample income to service a loan for the full value of the property. Their problem was security for the loan. Their $10,000 was well short of the 15% deposit, or $18,000, which the bank required for a $120,000 investment property. There wasn't even the extra they'd need for the stamp duty and all the etceteras.

"Sorry," said the bank manager most apologetically, "I know you can easily afford the loan repayments but I'm somewhat hamstrung by the rules and regulations of this bank."

This was like having a door slammed in their face. They had been with this particular bank for years, and with such high incomes, had believed they would have no trouble at all getting a loan — especially since the manager had often joked with them about buying their own house. But they decided to try again and made another appointment for the next day.

This time, they went armed with a series of questions. They knew they had more than enough income to cover a loan of $114,000 (they intended using $6,000 of their own money as a deposit of 5% and $4,000 for costs). So they just needed to get over the 15% hurdle.

They quizzed the bank manager about the 15% deposit required by the bank. Could they take out the extra cash on bank card? Could they get a personal loan for the rest of the deposit? What if they went somewhere else for a personal loan, then got the investment loan through this bank?

They found the bank was willing to finance the property with a 5% deposit of $6,000, *only* if they lived there. Then, if they moved out, the interest rate would increase. Ron inquired as to how long they would need to live in the property to qualify as owner occupiers. The manager smiled and simply suggested they go away and sleep on it.

They did, and the following day, put a proposal to the real estate agent. They explained they could only get finance if they lived in the property. The agent started to remind them that the contract clearly said the vendors could rent back their house, but they immediately told him that they only wanted to sleep there one night.

And the vendors agreed. The bank readily approved the finance, so everyone had a win on this one. Ron and Julie were only required to put up 5% deposit on the basis that the one night sleepover at the property qualified them as owner occupiers.

Author's note:

Ron and Julie are typical of many young couples who graduate from college or university and immediately gain well-paying jobs that enable them to easily service a loan for a property. However, with many years spent studying full time, they have no savings they can use as a deposit.

I wouldn't suggest the strategy that Ron and Julie used to everyone, but it shows that problems can be overcome by a little lateral thinking — or if you go away and sleep on it. Ron and Julie did so literally, and it helped them cross two major hurdles at their very first attempt to buy investment property. They discovered a way to turn mountains into molehills.

45. The valuer

In 1989 Mary and Glenn wished to buy more property but wanted to finance their new acquisitions through a different financial institution. Not that they were unhappy with their present one, but it had seemed at times that other institutions offered better deals. However, they struck a small problem with valuers and phoned me to air their concerns.

They wanted to release two properties from a current mortgage to use as collateral in the new deal. This should have been a simple procedure, they believed, as their properties had increased substantially in value since the last valuations six years before. And removing two properties from the mortgage should keep the loan-to-value ratio (LVR) at an acceptable level, using the three remaining properties as security.

But one property that was to stay as a security on the mortgage came in with a valuation of $60,000, almost 30% below the expected $80,000. Mary and Glenn were taken aback. Perhaps the 6 in the $60,000 was really a "typo" for an 8, or maybe the valuer had looked at the wrong property. Perhaps they had paid too much for the property to start with. Yet they didn't think any of these reasons were really the case.

They rang the valuer to find out the rationale behind this low valuation, but he would say no more than that he had done his homework well and his valuation would stand. Not only did it dent their confidence, it had an even bigger impact on their hip pocket. They couldn't remove the two properties from the mortgage unless they paid a substantial amount in mortgage insurance — $2,000! As Mary politely put it:

"We had four options. Pay $2,000 in mortgage insurance, leave a more expensive property on the mortgage, which we didn't want to do because it would upset our new deal, forget the whole idea of buying more property, or abuse the valuer and get an ulcer."

They chose to pay the $2,000, went on to buy more property, and sent the valuer a note wishing him well in his retirement.

Author's note:

Valuers have one of the most difficult jobs in the real estate industry. They are always in a "no win" situation. They are persecuted by investors if they undervalue, or prosecuted by financial institutions if they overvalue. To look at it objectively, they have far less to lose if they undervalue your property. Then it's no skin off their noses if they are wrong.

Mary and Glenn have learned to live with the fact that properties rarely value up to expectations. The irony of the story is that within only weeks of the episode, the property right next door to their "undervalued" property, identical in all respects to theirs, sold for $85,000.

Further note:

For those who are interested in the technical side of why the property valuations were so critical to the refinancing proposition, here is a more detailed explanation.

Five properties were held by the first institution, two of which were to be removed from the mortgage. The mortgage had stood for more than six years and in that time, property values had increased quite substantially.

The loan was for $225,000 but the properties mortgaged were estimated by Mary and Glenn to be worth around $560,000, giving a very low LVR (loan-to-value ratio) of 40.2%.

Thus, Mary and Glenn calculated that if they removed two of the more expensive properties from the mortgage, each valued at about $130,000, this would give them maximum leverage with the new financier, enabling them to buy the block of units they had in mind. These two properties posed no valuation problems.

It was the three least expensive properties to be left on the mortgage that caused their problems. As based on the new valuations, there was insufficient collateral remaining to maintain the new LVR below the 80% limit, above which the maximum in mortgage insurance would have to be paid. The three properties to remain on the mortgage and their valuations, according to the official valuer engaged by the bank and as estimated by Mary and Glenn, are listed below.

Valuations and LVRs

	Bank's Valuations	Mary & Glenn's Estimates
1	$125,000	$125,000
2	$95,000	$95,000
3	$60,000	$80,000
Total	**$280,000**	**$300,000**
LVR	**80.3%**	**75.0%**

From this table, you can see how critical the valuation of the third property was to Mary and Glenn's plans. That third property, if valued at $80,000, gave an LVR of 75%, which would have been well below the critical 80% at which mortgage insurance would have been needed.

With a value instead of only $60,000, the LVR was lifted to 80.3%, just above the critical level, necessitating the payment of the mortgage insurance.

10
Adversity to opportunity

In the previous chapter you saw how different people reacted to quite different problems. Some coped, some didn't. For those who did, it was simply a case of looking on the positive side of an incident, rather than on the negative.

But sometimes a problem can be completely turned around, so that adversity can become the opportunity to go on to bigger and better things. If you've got termites in a house and it's going to cost a lot to get rid of them, that's a little bit hard to do. All you *can* do is put the problem into perspective and consider how much money you have already made from that property.

However, while collecting stories for this book I came across many instances where people had been faced with serious problems, bordering on catastrophic, with the potential to cost hundreds of thousands of dollars. Yet they not only dealt with the problem, but actually used it to their advantage.

A very close friend of mind who has a wonderfully optimistic nature once told me:

"All my opportunities have come disguised as problems."

In reading the following stories, I hope that you too will be able to either put your problems into perspective, in other words, turn mountains into molehills, or to look on them as opportunities in disguise. There will be times when you must look hard, work hard, and think hard to see the opportunity — but it will be there.

46. The race

Merle and Murray started buying properties in the late 1960s. Their strategy was to buy something rundown, live in it, fix it up, sell it and then move on. They always spent a lot of time and money to make their properties very saleable, and took great pride in the finished product.

In 1973 Merle and Murray bought an old house for $9,000 with the same idea in mind. This time, the house was more of a shell. There were few internal walls, just a couple of very large rooms; no internal wall linings, no floor coverings and no stove.

For the next two years they worked countless hours and spent many dollars building dividing walls to make further rooms, adding wall linings, laying floor coverings, installing a hot water system and upright stove, and painting inside and out until it looked magnificent. They often stood back to look at the house and congratulated themselves on the great job they had done with this one. Then they put it on the market.

After receiving several offers on the property, Merle and Murray finally accepted an offer of $20,000 and proceeded to look for another old house to do up and again, to sell. However, in the course of the settlement they found that their beautiful house which they had devoted so much love, money and time to, was to be demolished. They felt devastated. They couldn't bear the thought that their masterpiece would be torn apart by a heartless demolition team and taken away to the dump.

The buyer had bought the property with the sole intention of building units on the site, which had been zoned for multiple dwellings. He had to get rid of the house, he was only interested in the land.

Merle and Murray asked him if they could have their house back — just the house, not the land; and he agreed, providing it was moved post-haste before he started building. This purchaser was a fast moving developer, so Merle and Murray, in a race against the clock, rushed around to find a house removalist and bought a block of land several streets away — all in record time. Within days, the house was moved to its new home, and Merle and Murray moved back in.

They eventually sold that house on its new block for $35,000 in 1976, and have since gone on to renovate many more properties, often shifting houses in the process.

Author's note:

Nowadays, Merle and Murray are property managers. In fact, they look after several of our properties and do so exceedingly well. I suppose it is understandable when you consider they are long-time property investors themselves and know the needs of both tenants and landlords first hand.

47. The NIMBYS

Dianne and Mervyn live in an inner suburb of Sydney. They came home from work one night to find a town planning consent notice board erected in front of the old terrace house next to theirs. The notice advised local residents of a developer's intention to build a multi-level complex of more than 130 townhouses.

A derelict old bakery was on the proposed development site, which had limited street access, so no one ever dreamed of anyone building there. But the developer had already solved the access problem by buying and demolishing two terrace houses.

The problem for Dianne and Mervyn was that their small terrace house would be surrounded on two sides by much taller buildings. To the north, the complex would interfere with their summer breezes and winter sun, and to the east, it would completely overlook their backyard and destroy their privacy.

Every evening when Dianne and Mervyn came home from work, they grimaced when they saw the sign. They envisaged the absolute worst possible scenario and thought of every possible problem this development might cause:

Towering buildings replacing the existing tall trees, no morning winter sun in their breakfast nook, no afternoon summer breezes on their patio, traffic jams in the street at all hours of the day, prying neighbours looking through their toilet and bathroom windows, noisy music blaring, problem tenants disrupting the normally quiet neighbourhood, drugs being sold on the street, drunks coming home late every night, devaluation of their own property, etc., etc.

At one stage, such was their anguish, they even contemplated selling up their home of ten years and moving out. How dare a developer do this to them! How could a council allow this to happen!

Feeling desperate, Dianne and Mervyn formed a local residents action group to try to block the project. They were not against development per se, as, being veteran property investors themselves, they had built up a considerable property portfolio including several townhouses. They were only against development on their own doorstep — in their own backyard, to be more precise.

After months of hopeless haggling with the developer and the local council, the development was approved and work commenced. The graders moved in, the trees began to fall and the dust started to fly.

Dianne and Mervyn watched the townhouses take shape, getting more and more depressed with every brick. Every evening when they came home from work they sat on the back patio and visualised who would be looking down on them in the not too distant future. Each weekend, they thoroughly inspected the building's progress to see if there was some tiny thing they could possibly use to halt construction. They were grasping at straws, but it was better going to a lot of trouble now, than putting up with all the problems later, they thought.

During one of these inspections they found, to their surprise, that the townhouses were to be well appointed, with luxurious fixtures and fittings. And each would have two lock-up garages. They also discovered there'd be a fully equipped gymnasium, a sauna and spa, swimming pools and a tennis court.

Their minds were set to thinking. Their terrace house had no off-street parking, their car being left outside in the narrow street astride the gutter. And, being sports loving people, they would travel miles to the gym, and even further to go for a swim or play tennis. They came to the conclusion that they might actually benefit, in more ways than one, by purchasing one of these townhouses.

And buy one they did! As owners, they could stipulate to the tenants that only one of the two garages was to be used. Dianne and Mervyn would be using the other one. And they retained the rights to have access to the gym, pool, sauna and tennis courts.

Author's note:

If you can't beat them, join them.

Dianne and Mervyn are very close friends and I was privy to most of the moaning and whining that went on over this development. Every time I visited, I was given a rundown of how the complex would impact on their lifestyle. I was shown the trees to be knocked down, the height of the building, the position of the windows, and anything else of note. So no one was more surprised than me when they told me of their intentions to buy into the complex.

Now, even better than having their own sporting facilities and garage, in the past two years the townhouse has increased in value from $220,000 to $340,000.

We are all NIMBYS (Not In My Back Yard) at heart. In England, they are called NODAMS (No Other Development After Mine). It's human nature. But Dianne and Mervyn didn't let what was happening in their own backyard destroy them. They found an opportunity in the gloom.

Don't sit around bemoaning the fact that something hasn't worked out quite right, make the most of every opportunity that comes your way. Sometimes opportunities do come disguised as problems.

48. Gran's legacy

A friend of mine in real estate told me this story about a middle-aged couple who bought an investment property almost three years after they first started looking.

Ray and Louise were in their mid-fifties, and their two children had long ago left home. On the day they paid off their own home they began to think seriously about investing. They had seen Louise's mother struggle on the pension for years and didn't want the same thing to happen to them. So they spent the next six months talking to financial planners, attending investment seminars of every kind, and even visiting the stock exchange on open day.

Having already lost some money in a "guaranteed" superannuation fund they wanted to control their financial affairs themselves, and settled on the idea of buying investment property. They liked the idea of buying units or flats, believing they would involve minimum upkeep, and their bank had tentatively approved a loan for $250,000, subject to valuations, which was enough to buy two or three such properties.

They searched for months and often were a hair's breadth away from signing a contract, but always pulled out. The problem, the agent soon discovered, was not the properties. They were fearful of taking on another loan. Ray was most apologetic in explaining to the agent why they just couldn't commit themselves:

"We can't go ahead. I'm sorry if we've wasted your time, but my wife is losing sleep over all this and I'm making myself sick with worry.

"We feel that taking on another loan after we've just got rid of one is like jumping over a cliff. Just thinking about it makes my stomach rise up my throat. I hope you understand."

So the agent, respecting their decision, backed away and left them in peace.

One evening many months later Louise received a phone call to say that her mother had fallen down the back stairs of her home and was being rushed to hospital. "Nan", as everyone called her, hadn't broken any bones, but it was now obvious to all concerned that she was getting frail and having trouble coping on her own, and would need extra care. She certainly couldn't return to her rented high-set house with its front and back stairs to live by herself.

After many sleepless nights worrying about what they might do, Ray and Louise decided that when Nan left hospital, she should come and live with them. But their house was also high set. The only solution seemed to be to build a granny flat underneath.

The plans were drawn up to suit Nan's needs, the council approved the proposal and Ray and Louise borrowed $40,000, easily qualifying for the loan. They were most unhappy to be in debt again after struggling for so long to get out, especially having just made a decision that they weren't going to borrow. Nevertheless, they were willing to make the sacrifice for Louise's mother.

They both breathed a sigh of relief that they hadn't bought any investment property. Otherwise they would have had the problem — as they saw it — of trying to deal with two loans at once, and so being forced to sell.

The building work went ahead without too much drama and inside four months Nan, with some of her more treasured possessions, moved in. But six weeks later, she died.

In the midst of her grief, Louise felt a flare of anger. How *could* her mother have died now? How *dare* she die now when they had just taken out this loan and spent all this money on her.

The anger lasted for only a brief time, and deep down, Louise was very grateful to have been able to do what they did. Within a few months, everything had returned to normal, but Ray and Louise did wonder what they would do with the granny flat.

In fact, a friend happened to ask them if they knew of a place where her daughter could stay while she was studying, so they rented the flat to the daughter. Ray and Louise put the rent money towards the $40,000 loan and in just over three years, had paid it off.

They soon came to realise that the $40,000 loan wasn't such a big deal after all, and with the extra rent from the granny flat, they could now easily afford another loan. More confident now, it didn't take long for them to start thinking again about buying investment property.

So they contacted the same agent, the one who had spent six months showing them around three years previously, and explained that they were now ready "to jump". He knew exactly what they meant, and this time, they bought a property.

Author's note:

Adversity had forced Ray and Louise to quell their fears about taking on more debt. Taking that first step with the loan for the granny flat was the hardest for them, and they certainly wished it hadn't happened the way it did.

But at least they made the most of the situation and now have no fears about borrowing to buy more property. Nan could not have left them a more effective legacy.

49.   Curse the council

Floyd is a commercial fisherman who worked hard throughout his seventy plus years. His wife Jess, while not having the same salt water in her veins, worked as hard on shore helping to process the daily catch and raise their four children. They often talked about retiring, but Floyd loved his work and couldn't imagine retiring to do nothing.

At the time of this story, they had lived for more than thirty years in an old high-set fibro house and run their fishing business from an ageing shed at the back. However, they badly wanted to move.

Jess was supportive of her husband's desire to continue in the business that kept him young and alive, but she longed for a new house with some creature comforts. Jess loved cooking and had her heart set on a new kitchen with a few mod-cons that most of us take for granted.

Also, they wanted to rid themselves of the problems created by two old flats they owned on the adjoining block. They were never really interested in investment property, but these flats had been built by Floyd's father many years ago, and Jess and Floyd had inherited them. The flats had been let at first, but the demands of family and professional fishing left little time for managing the tenants and keeping up with the maintenance, so that now the flats were empty, and besides that, somewhat of an eyesore.

Taking into account the problems of the flats, Jess's dream of having a smart, modern kitchen, and the fact that they were getting older and finding the steps tiresome, Floyd and Jess decided that the answer was to sell up everything and buy a new, low-set house with a big shed at the back for Floyd's business.

For three years they searched the area for a new, or near new house, with a suitable backyard shed. But what they were looking for didn't exist. And worse, when they tried to sell their house and land plus the flats next door they received no offers for anything more than the "land only" value of $240,000. The prospect of a developer demolishing the family home and the flats that Floyd's father had built was distressing.

At the same time, they started to realise that the money they'd been placing in term deposits for their retirement was unlikely to be enough, especially if they had to use some of it to buy land and build a new house and shed specific to their needs.

At a dead end and about to give up, they discussed their problems with their four adult children who came up with a suggestion. Since the two blocks of land were large and zoned Res B, why not build a new low-set house on one of them? Then Dad could keep his shed and Mum would have her new kitchen.

Floyd and Jess liked the idea. But not the council:

"No, you can't do that. This land is zoned Res B. You have to build multiple dwellings on a Res B block," the council officer told them.

"But we do want to build multiple dwellings. We want to add a house to either of the two blocks where there's a building already," Jess pointed out, trying to appeal to the officer's sense of compassion.

"It doesn't work like that," was the answer. "The rules and regulations for land zoned Res B are very clear. According to the town plan, you can have a house on each of two separate lots, but not two separate houses on the same lot. Other than this, dwellings must be built in pairs."

Curse the council! Floyd and Jess were ready to give up — again. But their children weren't going to let go so easily. They were now determined to go through the regulations with a fine tooth comb to find a way to allow Floyd and Jess to build their retirement home on their own land. They had watched Floyd and Jess get more and more depressed after having their hopes lifted when the idea was first mooted.

They thought of everything. One option could be to attach a new flat to either the old house or the flats, but this would be too costly with the major work needed to meet the new fire regulations. And anyway, who'd want to live in a new brick flat hanging off an old fibro building? Another thought was to build a new pair of flats at the back of the old ones, but separated as much as possible to provide some privacy. But Floyd and Jess didn't want to spend money from their retirement funds to build two flats when they only needed a single dwelling. Curse the council!

Months passed and after plenty of family deliberation, Jess and Floyd decided their best bet from a terrible set of options was to build two new flats behind the existing old ones next door. Plans were drawn, council approval obtained and construction started. They were also persuaded to spend a few thousand dollars to refurbish the old flats and rent them out to supplement their income. Virtually on the day Floyd and Jess moved in, four sets of tenants moved into the new flat next door, the two refurbished "old" flats and the old house.

Two years later, Jess and Floyd reckon it was the best "move" they ever made. Jess has a nice new "house", Floyd has access to his shed, so he can continue fishing, and the tenants have all been the best of neighbours. Even better, the net rent from the tenancies is double the income they would have received had they relied solely on the interest from their term deposits. Thank you council!!

Author's note:

Sometimes we should be digging for diamonds in our own backyard.

50.   The main road

I recently met a husband and wife team of developers, Sven and Angie, who were looking for new ways to market their units. They understood the principles of investing in property and had kept quite a few of their units along the way. But just now, they were eager to find out how to market more effectively.

As we chatted, they told me a most fascinating story of how they had escaped a debacle when marketing one of their projects three years ago:

"We had just completed a development of 20 two-bedroom units in a project that was trouble right from the start.

"When we'd been looking for a suitable site for the units, there was not a great deal of choice. Other developers were flooding into the area where we'd been building for a long time, and most of the good sites were taken.

"We were forced to choose between moving into an area that we knew nothing about, or buying the only development site left, which was on a busy, getting busier, main road — in fact, the only main road in the area.

"In the city, we know that building units on a main road is not a real problem because just about every road is a busy road. Anyway, most people like the idea of having the bus at their door step.

"But where we were building was borderline rural/country, and the reason why people went there was to get away from the rat race and live in the peace and quiet — not to buy on a busy main road.

"But we took the punt that the area was changing and there would be at least some people who moved there who would want easy access to buses travelling to the city. So rather than go through a different council in an area with which we were not familiar, we bought the site on the main road, figuring it was cheap enough to warrant a small risk.

"But we were wrong. It was a very big risk.

"The year was 1995. The building industry was in a downturn and it was impossible to sell any units off the plan. Less than six months into the project we realised it was going to be impossible to sell any units at all, even when the building was completed.

"There were very few owner occupiers around, even though interest rates were continuing to fall, and even fewer investors. And those who did express a vague interest in units in that area were put off by the closeness of the main road. They wanted units in the peaceful backstreets, away from the drone of traffic.

"Everything seemed to be against us. We'd half expected it to happen, but we'd thought that if we could just sell a couple of the units, it would get us out of trouble. We were prepared to hang on to the remainder to keep as rentals for ourselves and sell them at a better time.

"We tried everything we could possibly think of to sell those units. We supplied detailed quantity surveyors' lists of building costs, fixtures and fittings to investors. We tried rental guarantees.

"Even the local real estate agents couldn't suggest an answer short of giving the lot away at a heavily discounted price. But we had already dropped the price from $140,000 to $120,000 and any more would mean we'd lose completely — and we had never lost on anything, ever.

"Then one of us (I say it was me and my husband says it was him, but I guess it doesn't matter who it was) had an idea. If the main road was the problem, how could we put it to use? The answer was easy — turn the units into a motel. But it was better than a motel. This must have been one of the first sets of fully serviced apartments to come onto the market.

"It took us three months of council wrangling to make the necessary zoning conversion, but we finally did it. In the end, when they understood it, the council was in full support, as they could see a huge potential to bring more tourists to the area.

"There was nothing we needed to do to the units themselves, except create a manager's office out of one. So you see, we were able to market the units in a completely different manner. The main road was now a great asset.

"We were able to put the price back up to $140,000, which compensated for the loss of the unit we converted for the manager. And for an investor, there was a much better yield of $10,000 net per year, instead of the $6,000 net rent achievable via permanent rental.

"But best of all, because the building was now classified as short-term traveller accommodation instead of a normal residential income-producing building, it qualified for the higher capital allowance of 4% instead of 2.5%, effectively giving the investor a price reduction of $10,000."

Author's note:

Over the years I have come across many developers who have struck problems in marketing their product. Sometimes it is the result of not doing enough homework, often it is caused by the unsuspected changing needs of society.

As people have met these changing needs I have seen offices refurbished as residential units, houses converted into offices, warehouses rebuilt into flats, petrol stations turned into fruit markets, and I'm sure you've seen more. I have even seen a water tower converted to a home and a windmill transformed into a restaurant.

11
Mind over matter

When my brother and I were young children, we were never allowed to get sick. My mother's very simple philosophy was that most illnesses were "all in the mind", so that if we convinced ourselves we were well, forgot about the pain and carried on as normal, we would be just fine. We were not allowed to stay home from school under any condition. Well, almost. If we were violently ill we were given an ultimatum:

"Go to school or spend the rest of the day and night in bed. No play, no radio (we didn't have TV then) and don't get off the bed, I'll bring the potty in."

It was up to us then to decide just how sick we really were. As a result, our report cards showed mostly zeros for the number of days absent. My mother's philosophy paid off. Not only were we never allowed to get sick, but strangely enough we never did. I have followed my mother's great philosophy throughout my life and have passed it on to my own children, with the same result.

I have found that the "mind over matter" philosophy carries into every other aspect of life. The older I get, the more I realise just how many investment decisions are psychological. And the dominant factor affecting our mind is usually associated with fear. Fear of failing. Fear of debt. Fear of doing something different. And fear of doing anything at all.

The following stories are about people who have been influenced one way or another by fear. Some have used it as an excuse for not investing. Others have overcome it, and others have never had it.

51. Full circle

I received a telephone call from a frustrated woman one Saturday night, asking for a private consultation.

"I'm sorry," I said, "but I don't provide that service any more. Perhaps you could get your accountant to go over your personal details."

"No," she said, "I want *you* to talk to my husband. To convince him to buy a property. For the past ten years I've wanted to buy property but he always has an excuse and we keep going around in circles, arguing. Could you please talk to him for a minute if I brought him to the phone?"

"I'm sorry, but I don't like coercing anyone into investment property. All I can do is present the facts as I see them and hope people will act."

But the caller was not deterred.

"But I know he wants to do something because he says he's worried about the future. I know he doesn't want to use a fund manager, and he says money in the bank is dead, and shares are not his cup of tea, but I just can't convince him to buy a property. Could you *please* spare just one minute to convince him?" she pleaded again.

"Look, I'll spare a minute to give you a few clues so that *you* can convince him, if that's what you want. Just ask him these six questions.

1. Will you have enough assets for a financially independent retirement?

2. Do you believe the Government will look after you when you retire?

3. Is there anyone else who will look after you when you retire?

4. Do you think money in the bank is a good investment?

5. Do you think you can pick the right shares?

6. Do you know anyone who lost money by keeping residential property in the long term?

"If he answers the last question with a series of 'but what if's', which is what you would expect from someone who is procrastinating, counter it with: 'But what if you don't?' Then go back to question one and go through it again. That's about as much as I can suggest. If he likes going round in circles, this is perfect."

Author's note:

I quite often hear about, or talk to a couple where one of the partners is rearing to go and the other is reluctant to do anything about investing in property. I have found that these simple questions often make it seem more logical.

52. The risk

A close friend of mine, named Pippy, mentioned to me one day that she and her husband were ready to invest in property, but they didn't want to risk the family home by using it as security for a loan.

"It seems so logical to use our equity to buy some property, and I fully understand how it works," she said, "but we've worked hard to pay off our home and put so much money into it that it would kill us if we lost it."

Pippy and Errol have indeed worked hard for their home. It started over 20 years ago, in 1976, when they borrowed to buy ten acres of land for $15,000 and lived there in a tin shed with their two children for the five years it took to pay off the loan. Their goal was to build a large home and live there for the rest of their lives.

They were so cautious, however, that they refused to take on the huge $30,000 construction loan before being free of debt. (The average cost of a house with land in Brisbane at that time was around $25,000, so the value of their completed home, at $45,000, would have been roughly twice this.)

They did build a large brick home in 1981, but building costs went up while it was under construction, rising more than 30% over a six month stretch. Pippy and Errol were owner builders, with no fixed price contract, so the cost of the house escalated to almost $40,000. They knew they'd have saved themselves a lot of money if they had started building earlier, but as Pippy said, "We would never have been able to sleep at night with two large loans."

They tried to pay off their housing loan as quickly as they could. Errol did as much overtime as possible at the meat processor's where he was a supervisor, and Pippy worked part-time as a clerk. It took them ten years to clear the loan, and then, for the next seven years, they ploughed every penny into landscaping and furnishing the house.

Now, in 1998, with nearly everything finished, they would like to be property investors. They have studied up on the subject and are convinced that buying residential property will give the greatest and safest returns for the next fifteen years, when they hope to retire.

But, unless they mortgage their own home and borrow the full amount immediately, they think it will be at least another three years before they have the money for a deposit. Yet they know what happened the last time they waited to do something — prices went up astronomically.

So Pippy feels she is in a dilemma, and you can appreciate why. They are very conservative people, and they built their family home through sheer grind. They were so cautious that they avoided having two loans simultaneously, yet it cost them a lot of money. So they can wait yet again, or re-mortgage. Rather than talk them into something they didn't feel comfortable with, I tried to explain the implications of mortgaging or not mortgaging their home:

"Life is one big risk. We run the risk of something happening to us every time we get out of bed. But it's important to weigh up these risks. We make judgements based on the likelihood of something happening, but it doesn't eliminate the risk altogether. It simply lessens the risk.

"For example. Would you rather drive to the shops in a car, or as a pillion passenger without a helmet on the back of a motorcycle? Either way you run the risk of having an accident, but driving a car is probably less risky. Even though there is still a risk, however small, it doesn't stop you altogether from driving your car to the shops. Does it?

"When it comes to an investment decision, there is another set of risks. Which one would you rather take — the risk of mortgaging your family home and finding you could lose it? The risk of waiting five years to save a deposit and finding prices have escalated? Or the risk of doing nothing and finding there is no pension when you reach 65 years of age?

"The risk of losing your family home because it's mortgaged to buy investment property is minuscule. The number of properties taken as mortgagee in possessions is small and the number relating to investment property is smaller again. Secondly, there is a *real* risk of prices moving by the time you've saved a deposit. And thirdly, with people living longer and the tax base dwindling as a result of our ageing population, there is an *enormous* risk that the age pension will eventually diminish, if not disappear altogether.

"Now, I don't want to frighten you, but to put it into perspective, there is the risk that you could lose your family home even if it's *not* mortgaged. Suppose you got into financial trouble through credit cards or the like and were to finish up owing the bank $20,000 with no hope of paying it back. This is highly unlikely to happen, but just suppose it did. You'd think your family home was safe because it's not mortgaged, wouldn't you? But the truth is, it's not. If the bank was insistent, they could obtain a court order giving them the power to sell your home, recover the debt and give you what remained — if anything — because they wouldn't care what it sold for in a firesale.

"So you see, the family home is always at risk. You just have to weigh up the facts of life and minimise any risks. Quite frankly, I believe doing nothing is the greatest risk."

Author's note:

Pippy and Errol did mortgage their family home and buy an investment property.

53. By the book

Not long after the "white book", *Building Wealth through Investment Property,* was released, a real estate agent I had come to know asked me when I was going to rewrite it. When I asked him why, he told me there were sections in it that some investors were treating as "gospel" and that he knew of one instance where a couple had missed out on an excellent deal because of this. So he told me the story of Tony and Cara and I realised they certainly had read one relevant line in the book, but not the paragraph.

Tony and Cara live in Sydney and three years ago a long lost aunt died in Brisbane leaving them a part share in a three-bedroom unit in Toowong, an inner suburb of Brisbane. The other beneficiaries, Phil and Leanne, lived in Perth and after thinking it over, they decided they would like the money from the unit to prop up their struggling business.

The unit was conservatively valued at $280,000 and Phil and Leanne offered their half share to Tony and Cara for only $100,000, as they were keen for the settlement to be completed as soon as possible.

Tony and Cara had been thinking about buying more property for a few years and could easily afford to borrow the $100,000 to buy out Phil and Leanne. They had even been to their bank, getting approval to borrow up to $350,000.

They flew to Brisbane the next weekend to check out the location of the property and to gauge from the local agents whether the public trustees' valuation of the unit was correct. In fact, they soon found it was closer to $300,000.

They also learnt that the unit would return almost $10,000 per year, net of expenses, providing a positive cash flow from day one, as the loan repayments on the $100,000 would be only about $9,000 per year.

As well as a positive cash flow there would be no hassles in finding a tenant as the unit was already tenanted, courtesy of the public trustee who had been managing the estate for a year until the beneficiaries of the will had been sorted out. Even better, the present tenants, who were on a short-term lease, were anxious to convert to a long-term one.

But after their weekend away checking every detail about the property and establishing that it probably was a very good investment, Tony and Cara declined the offer to buy out Phil and Leanne for the $100,000.

Why? Because Jan Somers said in one of her books that you should buy investment property within a 15km radius of where you live!

Within a month, the unit sold for $300,000. Phil and Leanne were ecstatic at receiving the extra unexpected windfall of $150,000 instead of the $100,000 they were prepared to accept, and they put the money into their business, which is now thriving. Tony and Cara were also delighted that they now had the opportunity to buy closer to their home in Sydney. They put their money into the bank while they looked around.

After a year they decided that properties in Sydney were too expensive. Using their $150,000 inheritance as a deposit, they would have needed to borrow a further $200,000 to buy a decent $350,000 investment property in the Cremorne area where they lived. But they didn't want to borrow this much, even though the property would have produced a positive cash flow.

So they spent most of the inheritance on a prestige car and the rest on a holiday overseas.

Author's note:

This story was beyond comprehension — even for me, and I've heard just about everything. I had to grapple with it for a long time to try to understand what had happened. In analysing it, I believe that when we are fearful of doing something, we seize on any little tid-bit as justification for not going ahead.

We hear the "throw away lines" that we want to hear and often miss the qualifying comments that follow. It's highly likely that Tony and Cara were more "gunnas" than they were "doers", and consequently remembered only that one "15km radius" sentence in my book. But the rest of the paragraph read:

Of course, this is not always feasible, particularly if you live in an upmarket area such as Sydney's North Shore. There will be many investors from both Sydney and Melbourne who must look farther afield to a different suburb of their city, or even interstate, to find appropriate rental property.

At one time or another we are all guilty of half-listening, especially when we have a fear of something going wrong. I well remember the time a few years ago when we were considering a material called Corian for our new kitchen bench top. The builder commented:

"I think it might stain with beetroot."

I was so shattered that I never "heard him" qualify it with:

"But now I come to think of it, that was some other material we used for a sink one time."

I immediately rushed home, opened a tin of beetroot, poured the juice into a cup and stuck in my sample piece of white Corian. A week later I pulled it out, examined it closely, and found there wasn't a hint of red stain on it. I should have listened to the builder's other remarks and not to my own unfounded fears which were clouding my decision making.

54. Toby

A man named Toby phoned me enquiring about my first book *Manual for Residential Property Investors*, after hearing it mentioned in a video. The book went out of print in 1989, but I was able to tell him that the contents had been incorporated in my later book, *Building Wealth through Investment Property (1992)*.

He explained he was a keen property investor trying to find out as much as he could before borrowing $250,000 for a property. I told him that it would depend on his assets and wages and that he would be best to talk to either his accountant or bank manager because I didn't provide a personal consultancy. But his reply threw me.

"I've got lots of assets — about $1,100,000 with only a $65,000 debt. But I'm worried because there was a time I was in 'bad' debt and ever since, I've had this fear of taking on loans. I'll tell you about it one day."

One week later, Toby wrote me a long letter detailing his inspirational story about how he developed such a fear of debt. This is his letter:

From my late teens until I was 37, I was a complete alcoholic. I drank myself stupid and was in and out of psychiatric centres for years. I saw more bar room floors and footpaths than I could ever count. It was Black Friday, July 13th, 1973 when someone dragged me, very reluctantly, to Alcoholics Anonymous. I had $3.95 to my name, I could barely get to work, and I was in debt for $5,000.

Going to AA was the major turning point in my life. I went every night for three and a half years. I had to learn how to give in to win. It didn't happen over night. It took a long, long time. After much anguish, I gradually regained my mental, physical and spiritual well-being with the encouragement and support of fellow recovered and recovering alcoholics. I also resolved to get rid of the debt, so I slept in my car for a time, and virtually lived on baked beans.

By 1978 I had repaid the debt and I bought my first big asset — a $55 fridge. I couldn't sleep at night with this big "investment" sitting in the room, and it wasn't just the noise it made.

I was lucky I found a great girlfriend whom I met in 1980 when I was two years sober, and she is now my wife. Her first husband had died of alcoholism and here she was with me. On his death she had been left their two units. She must have had a lot of faith in me not to sell these units and watch me "piddle it against a wall".

But I was a totally changed man and I was determined not to return to the gutter. Yet I still had this constant fear of being destitute and in debt and began to save money like it was going out of fashion.

By the mid 80s I had saved enough to buy a new car outright. But the Australian dollar was taking a belting and the $12,000 car I wanted, started going up by $1,000 a month, eventually reaching $24,000. This was the second turning point in my life. I thought to myself, this is crazy, and I remember saying to the car salesman:

'You'll never convince me a car is worth half a house.'

So with this money and a small loan, we bought a unit at Darling Harbour. I paid it off quickly and it doubled in value within two years. Encouraged by this, we put a deposit on another property in Swansea and paid it off in four years.

Then came the 90s and I lost my job and got a redundancy. With some of the money and a small loan, we bought another unit in Darling Harbour. We also spent $75,000 on shares at 67c each. They fell in value but I bought more to average the price. They were highly speculative forestry shares but I thought I could make a quick dollar and then put it into more property. Our units had done well and I wanted to have all my money in property eventually.

Those shares are now worth 3.5c each and that was another big lesson. I lost as much as I hoped to make and it confirmed my belief that it is important to have control over your assets. So now I just stick to property. Since then, we have bought a home for ourselves and another unit in Swansea. And as I told you on the phone, we own near on $1,100,000 worth of properties and have a debt of just $65,000. I guess you could say we're millionaires.

We don't really need any more properties. We are happy doing the things we enjoy — I'm keen on art and photography and we love going on holidays. My life now has a good balance.

But we have a tax problem and that's why I'm considering another unit for $250,000. We can borrow the lot, given our income. It's not that we earn so much — I now have a casual job which brings in $14,000 per year (the most I ever earned was $24,000 a year), and my wife earns $38,000 as a supervisor. It's just that we get so much in rent. But I'm still afraid of debt. The fear of being broke, cold and hungry and living in degradation and despair is something I never want to experience again.

Author's note:

You certainly have to admire the inner strength Toby must have had to drag himself out of the gutter to get to where he is today. I didn't want to interfere with his decision on the $250,000 loan except to work out that the after-tax cost of the unit was $87 per week. Then I left it up to him. For Toby, it was not so much a financial decision as an emotional one.

55.   Terry's insurance

I first met Terry at a family get-together in 1997. His mother Netty, a distant cousin of mine, was terribly concerned because he had just borrowed $150,000 for a second investment property. It was barely two years since he'd borrowed $100,000 for his first one. It wasn't so much the debt that worried Netty as Terry's attitude. She explained:

"He set up his own business three years ago and it's going very well, but he doesn't seem to have much in the way of insurance."

It turned out not to be house insurance she was talking about.

"The two houses are insured but he's not. He has no medical insurance in case he gets sick, no income insurance in case he can't work, no cash in the bank for an emergency, his mortgage repayments aren't insured and neither is his rent in case he has vacancies. Anything could go wrong and he won't be able to cope.

"I was pleased when he started to buy property because he works so hard and it's nice to see him invest it rather than squander it, but I keep thinking about Murphy's Law. How will he keep up with the mortgage payments if anything happens to him? I suppose it will be up to me or he'll lose the lot."

I'm well aware of Murphy's Law (see Story 25). It states:

Whatever can go wrong will go wrong, at the worst possible time.

Consequently I have always advised investors to be prepared for all emergencies. Keep some cash on hand, set up credit lines and take out the appropriate insurances just in case you do lose your job. So I understood Netty's concerns and offered to have a quiet word with Terry when the opportunity arose.

I had no intention of interfering but it helps to try to understand the other point of view. Perhaps he had covered himself unbeknown to his Mum. Perhaps he had something up his sleeve for a rainy day. In fact, later that afternoon Terry approached me.

"Mum's told me all about you and your properties. I'm keen to do the same if I can. I've already got two and I really want to get another one as soon as possible. Any ideas on how to make it happen sooner rather than later?"

So we had quite an interesting conversation about property in general. As it turned out, Terry was just about ready to buy his third. He had already paid $70,000 off his original $100,000 loan and hoped to pay it off completely by the end of the year. He planned to buy as many properties as he could and retire before he reached 40. At the rate he was going, I could tell he was right on track.

We never did get to talking about insurance as such but it didn't matter. Terry had told me enough about himself in half an hour for me to conclude that he really didn't need any insurance other than house insurance.

He was an extroverted twenty-three year old with the confidence and poise of a seasoned businessman twice his age. He had completed a business management course at the Queensland University of Technology in 1994 and was heavily into marketing — anything. Right now he was marketing office supplies from his mother's garage, but as he said:

"If office supplies stops being the flavour of the month, I'll just start selling chook manure."

The more I talked to Terry the more I understood that he really did have something up his sleeve for a rainy day. His best insurance was his own mindset — his own personality.

Author's note:

I am often asked by investors about the kinds of safety valves they should set in place to ensure that their property investments run smoothly.

"How much income insurance should I have? How much cash should I have in the bank for each property? Should I have rent insurance? Life insurance? Medical insurance? Business insurance? Should I insure my mortgage repayments and for how much? Should I have...?" And the list goes on.

The truth is that there is no set amount for any type of insurance. Each one of us has what I call a "risk profile". At one end of the scale is the person who must have $10,000 cash on hand for every property they own, credit line access to a minimum of $500,000, life insurance worth at least $1,000,000, comprehensive income insurance, rent insurance and any other type that the insurance companies can think to offer.

At the other end of the scale is Terry. He had few insurances of the recognised type because he believed so strongly in his own ability. Terry is the sort of person who could get another job tomorrow if he lost his job today. He could start another business tonight if his current one failed. And he didn't have any cash lying around because he was paying it all into his loans at the rate of knots and he knew how to get it back if he needed to. In fact, he had built up sufficient equity in his properties to facilitate a credit line to cover any short-term liquidity problems.

And myself? I'm probably somewhere in the middle. I have always considered myself a very conservative investor. So I set up several credit lines before I need them and generously insure our properties and ourselves. As for the rest? My ability and my assets provide me with every other type of insurance.

12
Education after school

It was instilled into me that a good education was the key to financial security. The message from everyone was clear. Go to school, get a good job and you'll be set for life. If this message was right, then you'd have to wonder why, according to the 1996 Census, just 4.7% of the population retire with an annual income of $30,000 or more, the income that most people say they will need for a comfortable retirement (Perpetual Funds Management).

The "you'll be set for life" part of the rationale seems to have got lost. The fault lies with the reality that no one was taught in school how to set themselves up financially for life.

Our education system focuses more on teaching people the skills to get a job to earn money. It neglects to give people the opportunity to learn the money-management skills which enable them to manage their financial affairs. It is this skill which ultimately leads people to long-term financial security. Robert Kiyosaki, author of the book *Rich Dad, Poor Dad (1997)*, agrees and explains:

> The main reason people struggle financially is because they have spent years in school but learn nothing about money. The result is that people learn to work for money but never learn to have money work for them.

The following stories give credence to the fact that while conventional schooling is very important, it is not necessarily a passport to wealth and that real life education begins *after* leaving school.

56.   The economics lecturer

Phil is in his sixties and a university lecturer in economics. He is an expert on government fiscal policy, GDP and J Curves and can quote the monetary theories of Keynes off the top of his head. He has spent several sabbaticals overseas studying the economies of many other countries and is considered to be a world authority in his field. His reputation is such that his friends and colleagues often ask him for advice about their businesses or investments.

Phil's wife Barbara is 57 and is also tertiary educated with a Masters degree in mathematics. She was a high school teacher for many years, which was how I got to hear their story. They have two children, both of whom are at university, one doing engineering, the other medicine.

Do you get the picture of the family? Highly educated, the epitome of success in the academic world, and well respected in the community. They live very comfortably in a large luxurious house and have about $300,000 in superannuation.

But with retirement approaching, Phil and Barbara have just realised that their super will not be nearly enough for them to continue to live in the manner to which they have become accustomed.

Phil and Barbara had never thought much about retirement, believing that their academic qualifications would automatically ensure that their future would be OK. Somehow, the fundamentals of world economics and their own personal finances seemed to be very different.

They have begun to take stock of what they own — or more to the point, what they don't. Their home, worth $400,000, carries a $250,000 mortgage. Their beach house, where they entertain friends and Phil goes to write, is worth $200,000 and is mortgaged for $150,000. Their imported car, valued at $120,000, still has a residual on it of $60,000. And their super, which has always seemed so much on paper, is not even enough to cover the loans on their houses.

Phil and Barbara realise they must do something extra for their future. But selling one of their houses or even their car would cause them to lose face with their admiring friends, the ones who thought they knew so much about finance. So when Phil retires from his university post, he will be looking for work as an international financial consultant, hoping to reduce their debt.

Author's note:

Sadly, Phil and Barbara believed they knew everything about money. Too late they came to the realisation that an education — even one in economics — is not an automatic ticket to wealth.

57. The lesson

In the late seventies, my husband Ian was transferred to Sydney with his job. Having rented in Sydney five years earlier, we thought we would be more settled this time if we bought a place of our own.

We had a few properties in Brisbane at that stage, as I have mentioned before, but with prices in Sydney almost double those in Brisbane, we reasoned we would need to sell two properties to buy one. Also, we had no cash for a deposit as we had been trained from childhood to be debt free and had channelled all our spare money into paying off our loans — to such an extent that, at that point, we had very little debt.

Nevertheless, with our hearts really set on buying, we decided that if we found something we loved, it was worth the effort to sell two Brisbane houses. Otherwise we would rent.

On a cold, rainy afternoon I was out house hunting when I walked into an estate agent's office in Caringbah. I explained that my husband and I were looking for something to possibly rent, or preferably, if we could afford it, to buy, and I gave him a rundown of the properties we owned in Brisbane. He listened intently and then he casually said:

"Lady." (I was often addressed as just "lady" whenever a man was telling me something he thought any man would know as a matter of course.) "Lady," he repeated, "with what you have in Brisbane, you could afford to buy four properties in Sydney, not just one!"

And he went on to explain negative gearing — it was the first time I had heard the term — and how we didn't need cash, nor did we need to sell any Brisbane houses because we could mortgage them to buy in Sydney.

"Oh?" I said rather sneeringly, thinking of all salesmen everywhere as an uneducated bunch. What would a real estate salesman know that I didn't, when I'd been to university, taught financial maths at school and had a husband who was a university graduate in computer science? "I'll talk to my husband and get back to you."

I did talk to Ian and we decided that real estate salesmen would probably tell you anything to get a sale and couldn't possibly know anything about finance, so we ignored his advice and the next day rented a flat.

Author's note:

It wasn't until three years later that the penny finally dropped and I worked out that you could indeed buy properties without selling existing ones *and* without a deposit. I now have no doubt that the "uneducated" agent who gave me a lesson on that wet afternoon twenty years ago knew as much about finance and property as I know today — and neither of us learnt it at school.

58. The computer guru

A few years ago I received a call from Greg, a computer guru with a PhD from a prestigious American university who was working for a large insurance company in Sydney. His job was to develop financial models for the evaluation of annuity payouts and the estimation of future costings for life insurance and so on.

Here I should tell you, I'm not a world expert in either computers or mathematics. When I drew up a very basic spreadsheet on investment property cash flows more than ten years ago, it was to help me understand how we had managed to do so well in accumulating the properties we had, given our very average incomes. All I did was spend a few days producing the layout, while Ian spent many months programming the functions.

So I felt a little in awe when Greg, after introducing himself, said he wanted to ask me some questions about our PIA software.

"I'll try to help," I told him, "and if I can't, I'll put you on to Ian."

"When my young secretary showed me a printout from your software, I couldn't believe the figures were right. I'm 46, with a PhD in Computing. I specialise in financial models for the insurance industry and I truly never believed I could afford to buy a $200,000 property in Sydney.

"But here was this spreadsheet showing it was only going to cost me $50 a week. I couldn't believe it. I had to sit down, construct the financial model and write the program for myself.

"I managed to reproduce every number on the spreadsheet, including the $50 a week, so I have come to accept that it's true. But I can't seem to reproduce the Internal Rate of Return precisely."

So it wasn't an impossible question for me on programming. I briefly told him why the IRR (Internal Rate of Return) in our PIA calculation might have been slightly different to his and that Ian would send him a detailed calculation if he wanted one.

Having established its credibility for himself, Greg then bought our program because, as he said, he didn't have the time to re-create all the program's features. Greg is now an avid property investor who bought his first property the very next day and is already lining up for his second.

Author's note:

Greg and I chatted for some time about how it had been possible for him to have degrees in financial modelling, and yet be so naive in his personal financial matters. We agreed that something must be lacking in an education system that can produce such highly qualified people, who are often no better off financially when they retire than anyone else.

59.   The barman

When I first spoke to Steven four years ago he was wanting to get hold of our video on property investment. He asked me if it would tell him everything he needed to know about investing in property. I advised him my book would probably be better because it contained more detail, and the video was designed more for people to show to their spouses or children, or in fact, anyone who wanted to know the basics but didn't have enough time to read.

Sheepishly, he confided that he couldn't read too well so he'd buy the video. He then told me his remarkable story of how he had bought his first rental property when he scarcely could read or write at all!

When Steven left school aged just 15, his school inadvertently (but probably knowingly, says Steven, because they were glad to get rid of him) put his age at 16 on his reference.

Although he was barely literate he was a self-starter, and he'd decided that first and foremost he wanted to buy a car. He had always loved cars and often drove his father's around the country roads. Knowing he would need a steady job to qualify for a car loan, he approached several businesses in his local farming area for work.

He looked older than his 15 years and his brawn was enhanced by trips to a gym. (Later he told me that, to save on gym fees, he rigged up a home gym from heavy machinery parts from car wreckers.)

He had no trouble getting a job as a farm labourer, working from dawn till dusk, but he knew this was insufficient. So he applied for a second job at the local hotel as a night barman. He had no idea how to pour beer, let alone tell the labels on bottles and kegs, and the hotel was looking for experienced staff. But he offered to work unpaid for a week to learn.

The manager took him on and by the end of the first week, he could competently "pull a beer" and "draw a head", and had memorised the labels.

He soon saved $5,000, but was advised by every bank, building society and finance company in town that he was too young for a loan. And of course he couldn't fudge his age — they wanted much more documentation than his school reference. Undeterred, Steven resolved to work his butt off for the next year to save another $5,000 to buy his beloved car without the need for a loan.

He did it in six months and paid $10,000 cash for a rather loud, souped-up Falcon. However, as he was still sixteen, he had no driver's licence. He would be eligible in two months, so he enlisted his younger sister to help him read and memorise the driver's handbook. He passed the test so easily that he enrolled in literacy classes at the local community centre, studying for an hour at a time between his daytime farm job and going to the hotel at night. Within twelve months he had improved so much he was able to read a newspaper for the first time in his life.

By the time he had turned eighteen, Steven had saved a further $10,000 and was about to upgrade his car when the hotel manager suggested he should think seriously about buying a house instead. At the time, Steven told me, buying a house was the furthest thing from his mind. Wasn't it something you thought about when you wanted to settle down and have a family? Steven didn't even have a girlfriend, let alone plans for a family.

But he *was* keen to get ahead. He had proved to himself that he could get a job when some of his friends couldn't; he had learnt to read and write even though he had failed at school; and he'd bought a car though he was refused a loan. So he thought he could probably meet this new challenge and buy a property.

Mal, the hotel manager, convinced him he could do it and took the time to explain how easy it would be if he continued to live with his parents and rented the house out.

Steven forgot about upgrading his car and started saving more. He had reached $35,000 by his twentieth birthday, when he applied at a local bank for a loan of $50,000. Mal was most impressed with his young employee's attitude and gave him a few pointers about what to say at the interview — he even loaned Steven his best suit for the occasion. A far cry from the farming dags Steven had worn when he was just fifteen and looking for a car loan. Needless to say he got the loan and bought his first investment property.

When he phoned me, he had reduced the $50,000 loan to $20,000 in less than three years and was planning to buy another property as soon as he could.

"I'm still just a bit slow at reading," he said. "That's why I'll take the video."

Author's note:

Steven told me that, in retrospect, he wishes he hadn't spent his first $10,000 on his car. But I pointed out to him that he had learned some valuable lessons as a result of his sheer will to achieve his goal. Not only had he learned the skills of saving money, but it had also given him the motivation to learn to read and write.

Currently, Steven is a full-time trainee manager at the hotel. He not only reads and writes well, but is handling the accounts for Mal. Like many successful people, his real education began *after* he left school. There's no question that knowledge is the key to success — but you don't learn everything at school.

60. The FMC club

I have often found that property investors who have the opportunity to belong to a group are more likely to stay committed and succeed. The group is usually a loose band of people who meet informally at work, at sport or through some other common interest. They meet often, though not specifically to talk about property, but the topic usually arises. It gives them a great forum to talk over their problems and they can share their highs and lows. This type of interaction is one of the best forms of education. How these little groups work is highlighted by this letter I received some years ago from Matt.

Thank you for your excellent books. What I am about to reveal in this letter should give you cause for a little self congratulation.

I work shifts in the oil industry. I have always been keen on the idea of property as an investment and used to dabble in a block of land here and there. They were mostly only good for growing grass and weeds.

Late in 1992, a colleague told me he had a book that I might be interested in. He loaned me your book, *Building Wealth through Investment Property*, on the proviso that I browse through it for that shift only, which was 12 hours long. This meant that I had to read it between jobs that had to be carried out. I'm sure he thought that if I took the book home he would never get it back!

He said that if I felt serious afterwards about being involved with investment property, I had to buy my own copy. I knew he had recently purchased a property, so I was interested. The book was great. I couldn't put it down. So I went to town later and bought my own copy.

Soon after, in January 1993, I bought my first property using your principles. (Actually it was my 13th but I had sold all the blocks of land after making nothing.)

When I told my work mate about this he was over the moon for me. It was like I had just received the keys to a very special club. He then told me of other colleagues, who I'd never suspected, who had bought investment properties. One of them owned 5 units. He'd never talked about it, he drove an old car and he seemed just your average worker.

We call our club the FMC — Future Millionaires Club — and everyone is a blue collar worker.

One day, another workmate, who is rather conservative, asked us what we were all talking about so secretively in our lunch hours and he was given the same advice. 'Here's a book and if you like what you read, buy it.' He too became a member.

There are now five of us at work in the FMC. We don't volunteer information to anyone else. If someone is serious, we point them in the right direction — first buy the book. If they should then buy a property, we give them some advice and help them become aware of any pitfalls. And together, we are learning a lot more than we possibly could by ourselves.

There have been one or two others who have shown some interest, but they haven't bought a book. We believe that if they are truly interested, they should at least do that. Yet in the next breath, they talk about four wheel drives, stereos, boats, and so on. Then they grumble about how badly off their parents or in-laws are on the pension. They don't seem to be able to put two and two together.

And human nature is a funny thing. Some are cynical and hope that we crash. It is beyond their reasoning to understand that we can only crash as far back as where they are now.

Our group now has 18 properties worth $1,440,000 between us, at an average value of $80,000 per property. What each of us has is achievable by most other people.

I never believe in being smug about anything, as pride goes before a fall. But I lend myself a little bit of smugness now and then, as at the age of 13, my family and I were thrown out into the street in the pouring rain with nowhere to go. Our rented property was to be pulled down to make way for a development. I can assure you it is no fun sitting on the footpath with your possessions around you.

Thank you for your time in reading this.

Author's note:

Matt's FMC club is still going strong. Whether beginners or experts, we can all learn from other people. Often, people who I know are highly successful property investors come to my seminars, just in case there's something else they can learn. I also attend many seminars and enjoy talking to other investors for the same reasons. You may only learn one thing, but it could be worth a million dollars.

Where do you find such groups of people? Who knows. As you have already seen, it could be shift workers in an oil refinery. Maybe there's a group where you work. One thing is for certain, though. You must make sure the group you mingle with is positively going your way or you could find yourself in a mental rut if you happen to link up with a mob of do-nothing whingers.

13
You just never know

I'm sure that we've all been fooled by people, no matter how much we've thought we knew about them. This touches on something I wrote in my earlier book, *Building Wealth through Investment Property*:

> Our ideas of wealth are based on false assumptions that we "learn" in early childhood. We are led to believe that wealthy people must *look* rich and that people who *look* rich must *be* wealthy. Nothing could be further from the truth. This mistaken belief that wealth is manifested in external appearances is the reason we love to surround ourselves with the trappings of wealth in the hope that we will appear wealthy. Nice clothes, luxury cars, grand holidays and expensive furniture are all too often mistaken as a signature of wealth.

How many people do you know who appear wealthy and yet own nothing? Their designer suits were bought with plastic money and their flashy cars with personal loans.

If we can be wrong here, we can also be mistaken about the woman shopping in the supermarket dressed in shorts, floppy T-shirt and thongs. A battler? Someone on welfare? She could be me!

External appearances may be an illusion, not a reliable indicator of real wealth. Here are some stories about deception. As you will see, property investors can be those people whom you least expect to be, and at the other end of the scale, well dressed business people can own nothing when you wouldn't think that would be so. You just never know.

61.   The part-time cooks

Some of the letters I receive don't strictly constitute a story, but they touch my heart, particularly when they are about people who are average, everyday, in everyday, average jobs, doing things you wouldn't think was possible to get ahead in life. This was one such letter, from Hilary.

You'd certainly be proud of a small group of girls employed in the kitchen of our local Aged Care complex in Victoria.

We all work part-time on weekends to supplement our household income, and choose to stay at home and raise our young children during the week. Between the three of us, so far we have seven children and nine properties.

Being the youngest of the three (26) I was first inspired by Kay and Rhonda. Kay, who has three children, has been a property investor for several years and has a total of four properties. Kay and her husband choose to purchase older houses and renovate them, doing most of the work themselves, and then move on from there.

It was the introduction of your two property books by Rhonda that got me moving in the direction of property investment too. She has two children and three properties, one of which is at present being built in Queensland. Her future plans include purchasing more property and eventually retiring up north.

I only have two properties at the moment but they certainly won't be the last. Your books have been beneficial to all of us and every weekend we discuss aspects of your vast research and exchange advice and try to solve problems.

The future sure looks bright for three girls who are just part-time cooks and I'm sure that in the not-too-distant future, each of us will have a happy retirement.

Author's note:

When I contacted Hilary a short while ago to see how the group had progressed, she was very excited to tell me they have continued to have children and invest in property. Between them they now have nine children and twelve properties. Who would ever have guessed?

It just goes to show that you can never really tell which person is likely to be a property investor. It could be the electrician who comes to your house to re-wire your oven, or your garbage man; the girl behind the snack bar making your lunch-time sandwiches, or your handyman. It could be your kid's school teacher, or the family doctor or dentist. Or a part-time cook like Hilary.

62. The painter

Winnie rang me one day to enquire when I was next doing a seminar in Sydney. I told her it would probably not be for six to eight months as I was cutting down on seminars while writing this book. She wanted to know what the book was about and when I told her it was a collection of stories relating to property investors, she said:

"I have a story about a property investor, but it's not about me and it's not about finance or anything like that. So it mightn't be interesting."

I said I'd love to hear about it just the same. "You just never know what might interest other people." And so she began:

"It's about our very first experience with investment property. It was a simple little thing that happened but it certainly made me look at every person I meet in the street in a different way.

"My husband is a doctor, and most of his doctor friends own property, so I had always believed that investment property was bought by wealthy professionals. I'm not sure why that was. Perhaps it was because we only mix with the medical fraternity.

"The first place we bought for investment was in a sorry condition. It needed a lot of work so I organised for some tradesmen to look over it to see what needed to be done. One afternoon after surgery, we met the painter, Dan, at the house.

"He turned up in an old ute with his wife in the passenger's seat and two scruffy dogs running around in the back with the tins of paint. He explained that he was on his way to pick up his two boys from football training and he only had twenty minutes or so to spare. I couldn't see where they were going to sit but I assumed it was in the back of the ute with the dogs and paint. I told him I was sure twenty minutes would be more than enough.

"Anyway, we explained to Dan that it was simply a rental property and we didn't want to go to a great expense straight away. He was obviously on the ball and in no time pointed out what needed to be done and what didn't.

"He recommended we not bother with any of the ceilings as they were in reasonably good condition, except for maybe in the bathroom and the kitchen, and to paint the rest of the house in semi gloss as it would be much easier to keep clean. He also suggested doing the inside first and the outside later after tenants had moved in, to save losing rent.

"I was impressed by his advice. By the things he seemed to know, I guessed he had worked on a lot of rental properties for people in the past. So we asked him if he knew of a good managing agent.

"He gave us a business card for a local real estate agency, with the passing comment that he did a lot of work for them and they specialised in rentals rather than sales.

"I went to this agency the next day and told them they had been highly recommended by Dan the painter. The principal smiled and acknowledged that he knew Dan:

'Yes, he does a lot of work for us. He owns half our rent roll.'

'Oh,' I replied, 'so he's in business with you.' I was beginning to understand why he would recommend this particular agency if he owned half the business.

'No, he owns half the houses on our rent roll.'

"I was stunned. I didn't dare ask how many properties they managed but with two people looking after the rentals I judged it was more than a hundred. And when I told my husband he couldn't believe it.

'But he's just a painter. A house painter. He couldn't possibly own so much,' and he just kept shaking his head."

Author's note:

I followed up this story and found out that in fact, Dan owned more than fifty investment properties, a mixture of flats, houses and units he had acquired in the area over more than forty years. He has been a painter all his life and spends half his time painting his own rentals and the other half painting the other half of the agent's rent roll. I guess you could say he paints all the properties on the rent roll.

Dan almost fits to a tee the description of a typical millionaire given by Stanley and Danko in a book titled *The Millionaire Next Door (1997)*. They are talking about Americans and they describe him as:

A 57 year old man, married with three children

Self employed

Involved in "dull-normal" business such as pest controller

Average annual income of $310,230

Home owner with average property value of $401,920

First generation affluent

Lives below means, wears inexpensive suits, drives locally made car

Works 45 to 55 hours per week

Invests about 20 percent of taxable income

We have this belief that wealth is manifested in external appearances, but this story goes to show that you just never know.

63.   The tin-pot agency

Since our first experience with managing our own property we have always used others, often spending as much time looking for a good manager as we do looking for a good property.

Five years ago, when one of the real estate agents who managed our properties for us retired, we had to find another one, so I began to ask around. I knew what to look for in a good manager and in *Building Wealth through Investment Property* I described the essence of this process:

This usually means finding a real estate agent who runs his rent roll as a business — not just as a sideline to his real estate sales.

So I began looking for an agent who specialised in rentals, and talked to as many locals as I could, asking if they knew a good one. Eventually, an electrician who was working on one of our properties suggested Merle's agency on the way out of town.

I knew this agency, so I looked at him with disdain. It was a tin-pot, two-bit place on the back road, one we had driven past every other week for more than 20 years. I was always surprised to see it was still there. To tell you the truth, on many occasions I thought it had gone broke. It was just a tiny building in the front yard of a house with no shops nearby, and was only about four metres square — barely big enough to hold a desk, let alone run a business.

Expecting the name of a much larger agency I wasn't impressed with the electrician's advice, but nevertheless I made an appointment there for the next day, figuring I had nothing to lose. When I walked into the office it was even smaller than I had imagined, but I was immediately greeted by this friendly woman, Merle. After a few minutes of polite conversation I felt a bit more confident — Merle sounded as though she knew what she was talking about. And when she introduced me to her four staff who between them managed the rentals — all 500 of them — making them the second largest managing agency in the area, I felt very confident indeed!

Author's note:

There are many excellent property managers around, but who would have guessed that a first class professional operated out of such a small office in the middle of nowhere? Merle later told me that the local council had restricted their office expansion. Yet they were reluctant to move, because over the 20 years they had been there they had built up a clientele of excellent tenants who now sent their children and friends to the same small office. The postscript to this story is that with a change of heart from council, Merle's office is now ten times larger, and two months ago I went to the grand opening of their newly expanded premises.

64.   The developer

Howard is an expert on residential property. I know him well and have often talked to him about it. In the past 30 years he has developed, built and marketed more than 4,000 units. Although he had a team of architects, builders, finance experts and marketers, he had a hands-on approach and enjoyed the personal contact he had with his purchasers. Most of his units were sold to owner occupiers, with the remainder to property investors. Howard was able to assist most purchasers to such an extent that they came back to buy more units from him.

With owner occupiers, Howard showed them how to pay off their loans quickly. He believed that once they had, they would come back to buy more of his units as an investment — which many of them did. For the property investor, Howard would not only suggest the most suitable source of finance but he would give them a detailed report showing the anticipated cash flows of the property. He also provided them with a quantity surveyor's report of the fixtures and fittings in each unit, so that they could claim maximum depreciation in their tax returns.

So it came as a shock when Howard informed me one day that he never owned any units himself.

"You know, I'm an old man," he started, "and I've taught a real lot of people about investment property, but I never actually kept any. I know that's hard to believe, but I just didn't. One of my old clients was choosing a unit from my latest development when he asked me which units I was reserving. I realised then that I'd been too busy making money and spending it to think that what I taught everybody else actually applied to me, 'cause I was rich and my buyers weren't.

"I spent the lot. Sure, I have a nice waterfront home and a big yacht, but I don't have any other investments of note, just some cash in the bank. With me, it wasn't a case of practise what you preach. Do you know that if I'd kept one unit from every block I've built, I'd have more than 100 units today."

Author's note:

You would expect someone who markets investment property to also own it. But often it's the real estate salesman who knows so much about property who fails to have any of their own. It's the same in other industries. Have you ever noticed how it's usually the plumber's house that has rusty gutters or the painter's house that has peeling paint, or the paving contractor's house with the gravel drive? It's often the case that we are so busy making money, we neglect to look after our own interests. Howard was like this, but he is changing. He has since built two developments and has kept two units from each.

65.   The tattooed tenant

Glenda and her sister Margie bought their first investment property just over two years ago. They shared a small flat in the city and had figured that buying a property between them was at least a start since neither of them could afford to buy their own independently. As well, their own rent was comparatively cheap, so it made sense to stay where they were and get both the rent and tax benefits from their investment.

They planned the event thoroughly, even investigating the possibility of a pre-approved loan so there would be no last minute hiccups. They also decided that to be on the safe side, they would wait until they had at least a 30% deposit. By the end of the year they had increased their joint savings to $40,000, and proceeded to make appointments with real estate agents to start looking for something around the $135,000 mark.

After two months of looking at units, townhouses and houses, old and new, fastidiously getting all the detail on any that appealed, they selected a brand new house in a new estate for $140,000. It was a touch more than they had wanted to pay but it came complete with carpets and vertical blinds. The only thing that needed doing was the landscaping, but they figured this could be done without causing too much disruption while a tenant was in the house.

Everything went to plan. The finance went through smoothly, the settlement took place on time and they found a good property manager. They gave instructions to this agent to be particularly fussy with his tenant selection as this was not only a new property, but their very first, and they were still a little nervous about the whole process.

They shortly received a tenancy agreement by mail, which they duly signed and returned. Then one week later, when Glenda and Margie were driving past their house, they saw a motorbike parked in the carport with a heavily tattooed, pony-tailed young man playing around with the engine.

When he turned around to face them, after they had stopped in surprise, they could see he had rings in just about every place you could put a ring. Four apiece in his ears, two in each eyebrow and one through his nose, and wherever else — they hated to imagine. He just had to be a member of a bikie gang.

"Oh no!"

They were sure everyone on the estate heard their exclamation of horror. This couldn't be happening to their house, especially when they had told the agent who was managing the property to be exceptionally careful about selecting a tenant. They sped off up the road to his office, double parked the car and rushed in.

"Is that bull-ringed tattooed lout from Hell's Angels our tenant?" Glenda demanded, hoping he may just have been a visitor.

"Well yes," replied the agent meekly, "but let me explain."

"Explain nothing," chimed in Margie. "We want him out of our new house today — now — this very minute."

"Please let me explain," tried the agent again.

"It'd better be good!" snorted Margie in exasperation.

"This young lad happens to have excellent references."

"I'll bet they're forged," interrupted Margie again.

"I've checked it all out personally, because I couldn't believe it myself. I spoke to my very good friend and fellow agent John about Lee — he's your tenant — and John told me Lee is one of the best tenants they've ever had at his agency. I had to make sure we were talking about the same person and as soon as I mentioned the rings and tattoos, I knew we were. Anyway, John had a lovely letter from this guy's previous landlady.

"Apparently she was an old friend of the family and it turns out that Lee was kicked out of home when he was 13 and three years later, when he was old enough to get a job as a car-park trolley collector, this old family friend took pity on him and let him rent her small one-bedroom unit because she was going overseas. She gave the unit to John to manage so that at least someone could keep an eye on him.

"When she got home twelve months later, the unit was immaculate. Lee had even repainted the kitchen and bathroom, and landscaped her little courtyard. She hated to tell him he would have to move as there was no room for both him and her in her small unit. But she was so impressed with what he had done that she gave him most of her old furniture that she was replacing and the excellent reference.

"So there you have it. When he came to me, I thought he might be spinning me a yarn, but it's all true."

"It's just so hard to believe," exclaimed Margie. "We thought for sure he was going to dismantle his bike in our lounge room."

"I'll tell you what," said the agent. "If you're not completely happy when the tenancy ends in six months, I'll personally remove him."

Author's note:

I've also had tenants like this. As the saying goes, you should never judge a book by its cover. The agent who related this story to me later told me that Lee went on to landscape the yard for the sisters. He laid the turf, planted trees, did the garden edges and so on. He is still their tenant after two years and they hope he will stay indefinitely.

14
Spend to make money

My Nana always said:

"Look after your pennies and the pounds will look after themselves."

In part, she was right: we do have to save money. But there are also times when we want to spend it. Then we need to differentiate between when spending money is a waste and when it is an investment that can actually make us more money.

With property, this distinction is sometimes hard to determine. One disadvantage of investing in property for the long term is that it can be boring — *dead* boring — and so people tinker with their properties, just to keep it interesting and alive. They add an extension when they don't have to, put in spas that are not necessary, repaint the kitchen because they don't like the colour, and so on. It's a bit like adding an ashtray to the back of a motorcycle — it's money spent for no returns.

At the other end of the scale, cutting corners to save yourself money can turn into financial disaster.

These stories illustrate how attempts to save money in the short term have resulted in losing out over the long haul. Some of them relate to our own experience, when we've attempted DIY. Among other things, we have poured concrete, built carports, laid second-hand carpet, and painted houses. I liked learning something new and I liked to save money. I certainly did learn a lot, but in the long run, I didn't save much at all. Most things are worth doing once, to gain the experience, and then it is best left to professionals.

66. Polkadot carpet

Eleven years ago, when the carpet in one of our rental houses needed replacing, I decided I had the time to hunt around for some second-hand carpet. I pored over the local *Bulletin*, the *Courier Mail* and the *Trading Post*. After many phone calls and umpteen "I'll take a look" trips, I came across a bargain in the *Trading Post* for a cream, pure wool carpet imported from New Zealand, that wasn't yet 4 years old. On ringing, the sellers told me it was to be replaced because of a few small marks, and had to be taken away within two days as they were hosting a gala charity function at their place over the next weekend. So we decided to drive over and check it out immediately.

The house was in the most upmarket street in a very blue ribbon suburb of Brisbane. The carpet was also very chic and thick — I mean thick with a 4cm deep pile — and would normally have cost more than $300 a broadloom metre, an exorbitant price at the time. We spread out one of the ten rolls and saw a few marks which the owner assured us would clean off, and we bought the lot for $300 — an absolute steal, considering it had probably cost them well over $10,000.

We had borrowed a friend's trailer for the trip and loaded on the rolls, which I am sure weighed a tonne each. Next morning, with my tape measure in hand, I set about unrolling the pieces to match them to the rooms I had in mind in the rental house. To my horror, I realised that eight of the ten pieces had more than just a few brown marks on them — each piece had an array of bright orange polkadot patches on it about the size of a saucer. Or, suddenly remembering the dog I had seen at the house — the exact size of a poodle's piddle.

I rang the sellers straight away and their only response was that they were busy organising their weekend charity event and I could try dyeing the carpet. Stuck with it, I made enquiries about dyeing, but everywhere I asked, the answer was the same: the only way to hide the stains would be to dye the whole carpet either a deep indigo, or a very dark brown.

Of course an almost black carpet was not acceptable — even if it was 4cm thick. So on Monday, the day after the gala event, we loaded up the trailer with the carpet again and returned it. The sellers were so grateful we hadn't turned up during the function that they readily gave us our $300 back.

Author's note:

As well as learning a lot about attitudes, I learned about measuring and laying broadloom carpet. I decided it would have been cheaper to buy a modest but serviceable new carpet — which I did the next day. I have since bought very good second-hand carpet, but I make sure I roll out every piece and check for any additions such as orange polkadots.

67. The concrete mix

After concreting driveways in several of the various houses we'd lived in, we considered ourselves reasonably expert in laying concrete. So twelve years ago, when one of our rental properties needed a carport slab and driveway, we decided to do it ourselves.

We boxed up the 60 square metres, hired a bull-nose float, screed and helicopter and ordered the concrete for 7 a.m. the next day. When it arrived we quickly screeded it, but by the time we went to put the helicopter on the slab the temperature was up to 38°C and the concrete had set rock hard — all of this in less than an hour.

It was the hottest November day in more than thirty years and we had chosen it to lay concrete. Pushing the machine over the slab was like steel trowelling a gravel road. So the concrete was somewhat less than perfect, detracting from the place rather than adding to its value. It was so bad, in fact, that we had to call in a professional concreter to lay a further 25mm over the top just to give it a smooth, respectable finish.

Not to be deterred from laying concrete, we tried again a few years later when we wanted to put a solid flooring over the compacted rubble in the garage of another rental property. It was July, so we knew we wouldn't have any heat problems like the last time.

After organising the tools and the boxing we ordered the concrete for early one morning. This time, just to be on the safe side, we got it quite a bit sloppier to avoid it drying out too quickly, and consequently, it was very easy to screed and float. We then waited for it to "go off" so we could edge it and polish it with the steel trowel. We waited and waited, but do you think it would go off? Every time I set foot on it, my boot went through the slop to the bottom.

That day in Brisbane turned out to be the coldest July day on record, with a maximum temperature of just 9°C. This, coupled with the facts that the slab was under cover, was being laid on an impervious base, had brick walls on three sides and we had specially ordered a very wet batch of concrete, meant we were still there after midnight trying to trowel off by the lights of the car, as there were no lights in the garage.

Author's note:

There's not much I don't know about concreting now. But it would have been cheaper and easier to go to a tradesman's course at night school than to have made as many boo-boos as we did! Most of our concreting exercises have cost us much more than a professional concreter would have charged us, so we tend to use one nowadays. Besides, whenever we decide to lay concrete, it seems to cause extremes in the weather.

68.   The survey

Roly, a good friend, told me how he accidentally bought two properties. He was driving home from work one evening when he came across a traffic jam and decided to detour up a side street. At the front of a house he was passing was a "For Sale" sign. The house looked promising as it seemed to be on a large block of land, but he was driving too fast to get any details from the sign and it had no tell-tale colours or logos belonging to any of the local real estate groups. He made a mental note of the position of the house, deciding to check it out when he had the time.

The next Saturday, Roly returned to the house and found it was being sold privately. He took the details from the sign, which was hand written, and on phoning, found that the house belonged to a deceased estate and the son and daughter-in-law who had inherited it wanted to sell it privately to save on agents' fees.

The asking price was $250,000, but Roly noted that the land had two title deeds. However, the couple were convinced that the house was across both blocks, having contacted a surveyor who had come to assess and quote on surveying the land. He thought the house might just encroach on the boundary but his fee would be $1,200 to verify. The couple decided that the surveyor's opinion cost less than his services and didn't follow through.

Roly could see the potential of the property regardless of whether or not the house straddled the boundary and thought the couple would be keen to sell, as they had been trying to do so for more than four months. So he offered an unconditional $200,000 contract, which they accepted.

Roly took possession and promptly paid $1,200 to the surveyor — to find that the house did indeed encroach onto the second block of land, but it was only three sets of external awnings that overhung the boundary. Roly removed the awnings, freeing up the second block, and bought an old house, for removal, for $10,000. He then paid $20,000 to have it moved to the vacant block and restumped. Now, for spending that extra $1,200, Roly owns two houses worth $320,000, for an outlay of just $230,000.

Author's note:

This couple didn't see how they could make money by spending it. Firstly, they refused to enlist the skills of a real estate agent. It might be OK to sell privately if you know what you are doing, but just sticking a sign in the front yard won't work unless you spend money on advertising. Secondly, they did not appreciate the true value of paying a surveyor to make absolutely sure of the correct position of the house. In trying to save that $1,200, they lost many thousands of dollars. This is a classic example of how it pays to spend money on professional advice.

69. The salesman

Having an academic background, I naively believed in my younger days that people in real jobs were either well educated, white collar workers or hard working, blue collar workers. To me, there was no other category. Consequently, I saw people in sales as neither hard working nor educated, and always earning easy money at someone else's expense.

My attitude was such that I couldn't bear to spend money on anything where I suspected a salesman might make a quick, unearned dollar. My views on this have long since changed, but while they lasted they cost me dearly on several occasions. This story is about one of those times.

Early in 1976 we were about to buy our second property, in the Redlands area, just south of Brisbane. With advice from the bank that we could afford to spend $33,000 on a house, we started searching. (Indeed, both then and for the next five years we relied on banks to tell us what we could afford — see Story 39.) At last we found an ideal house for $23,000, but adjoining it was a vacant block of land on a separate title, which was also for sale by the same vendors for $7,500. We "ummed and aahed" for a few days about buying this too. It was not only well within our budget (or what the bank had established), it had views across Tingalpa reservoir — giving us a good investment and extra privacy.

We obviously chewed over the idea for too long, because when we were negotiating the terms of the contract on the house the agent informed us that the land had been sold. The purchaser had offered a seven day cash contract, whereas we would only have been offering a thirty day contract with a "subject to finance" clause. We were disappointed, but went ahead with the purchase of the house.

A month after we moved in, the agent who had sold us the house, appeared at the door one evening, enquiring if we were still interested in the land next door. I said we were, thinking that somehow the original contract must have fallen through, and the salesman went on:

"Well, the original purchaser has decided he doesn't want the land after all and he wants to give you first option."

"That's very considerate of him," I said quite excitedly. "How much does he want for it?"

"$9,500."

"But that's $2,000 more in just one month!" my excitement turning to disbelief.

"But it's worth every penny," said the agent. "$9,500 is probably its real market value. And the guy genuinely wants to sell because he's just got a job up in Townsville. He'll probably just break even."

"But you'll get double commission. Once for selling it to him and again for selling it to me." I was on the attack.

"Yes, but that's my job."

I immediately recalled my ideas about salesmen and how I believed they didn't have a real job and didn't deserve such rewards. So I silently vowed, he won't make as much as a brass razoo out of me, and neither will anyone else — not this two-timing salesman nor the two-bit vendor who beat us to the punch! So curtly I declared to the now retreating salesman:

"Thanks, but no thanks."

As the car drove off, I said to my husband, "What a hide! We're smarter than that!"

In that same week we bought a brand new car and a boat for $9,500. We did need another car, though not necessarily a new one, but with the extra money burning a hole in our pocket, we thought, why not? Now, more than twenty years later, that block of land is worth $90,000. And the car and boat? The car was towed away to the car cemetery many years ago and we virtually gave the boat away once the motor died.

Author's note:

This was a very valuable lesson — a $90,000 one. I was determined not to part with our hard earned money to help pay a salesman twice, but was prepared to buy a new car. Thinking back on the episode, I realise an irony — we refused to allow the estate agent to make money, but the salesmen who sold us the car and boat probably made just as much, we just couldn't see how much.

In time, I recognised that everyone is really a salesperson of one kind or another, even if they are not paid an actual commission. The girl selling cosmetics in the chemist shop has to be good at selling. The more she sells, the more her boss makes, the better he pays her. Young kids are the best salespeople. Have you ever noticed how good they are at selling you on the idea of having take-away when you had no intentions of buying it?

In a sense, the whole workforce is made up of salespeople and everyone is entitled to the money they earn. So don't make the same mistake that I did and believe that salespeople don't have a real job and are therefore not worthy of your dollar. Be prepared to spend money to pay people — even a salesman — to make more money for yourself.

Believe it or not, good salespeople in the real estate industry can be extremely knowledgeable (see Story 57), especially those who have made a career out of it. That's why they often call themselves consultants. They're also usually very sociable and can actually get just as much of a kick out of seeing someone else make money as they do themselves.

70. Up to scratch

A few years ago I was in Newcastle when a good friend who owns a lot of property contacted me and said:

"I'd like to run by you a little problem I have with some of my rental properties. Do you have a minute to spare?"

I have known Benny for many years. He is a lovely middle aged Italian gentleman who has worked hard all his life and has managed to string together quite a few properties. But he has never discussed any aspect of them with me, so I assumed that this matter, whatever it was, was of great concern to him. He explained:

"The problem is that I seem to be having a lot of vacancies with my houses at the moment. Two of them have been vacant for more than six weeks now. It never used to be this way. Do you think there's a glut of rental properties now?"

"Maybe your rents are a bit too high?" I suggested. "One sure way of attracting more tenants is to lower the rents."

"I've done that," Benny sighed. "I've even dropped the rent on one of the houses from $145 a week to $95 with no takers."

"Have you spoken to your agent about what the problem might be?"

"No, I don't have one. I'm not paying an agent to do what I can do."

"But with all the vacancies, what you're doing is plainly not working. If you enjoy managing them and have no problems, that's great. Myself, I'd rather pay someone to do it. It's tax deductible so it only costs you half what you pay. Would you consider asking an agent to take a look at the properties to see if they've got any suggestions?"

"Maybe, but I'd like to give it another few weeks first."

"I'll tell you what, Benny. Why don't you and I go for a drive to have a look at the ones you're having problems with?"

So Benny and I went for a drive around to look at his properties. The first one we came to was on the main road. I could best describe it as a one-bedroom shack with the bathroom and toilet separated from the main house by a covered alley way. There was no front fence, or back fence, and one of the side fences was falling over.

To open the front door you needed to lean on it, breathe the right way, then turn the key. Inside, there was daggy old carpet with a doggy poop in one corner. (The back door had no latch and was swinging wide open.) The oven door was hanging off the stove by one of its hinges, revealing the baked-on grease inside. None of the windows seemed to open easily and all the taps were dripping. I could go on.

"Benny," I said. "You need to get this place up to scratch. It's in such a lovely position with the shops just up the road that I'm sure it will rent right away if you just spend some money on it. To tell the truth, I wouldn't want to rent this place either. Am I right in guessing that the other properties you're having trouble with are pretty much the same."

"Yes, but I never used to have any trouble years ago."

"That may have been so. But these properties were probably in better shape then and anyway, tenants are more choosy now and want to rent something nice. With all due respect, Benny, I really don't know of anyone who would even think about living here. Would you?"

He tried to dodge his way around this question with a string of "buts".

"But it's just for tenants. But they'll only wreck it all again."

I could see he was going to go on and on and I didn't want to get into an argument about tenants. So I broke in.

"Benny, it's not a case of 'them and us', tenants are one of us. Just like you and me. We've all been tenants at some stage. My best advice to fix your vacancy problem is that you need to spend some money and fix your places up. There's no other way."

Author's note:

I don't want you to get the wrong idea here. In most cases, there's nothing wrong with a rental house being on a main road, or having one bedroom, or having the shower out the back or no fences. Most tenants are prepared to put up with at least some of these less desirable features. I know of a new house on a very busy main road and the tenants are always queued up to rent it.

The problem arises when *all* these minor deficiencies and damaged fittings exist in the same house at the one time and the landlord refuses to fix them.

An investment in property is an investment in your future, so don't let your rental properties become rundown. Sometimes, if a property is in bad condition, no amount of rent reduction will entice reasonable tenants to rent it. Keeping vacancies to a minimum is a combination of keeping the property well maintained and the rents at a reasonable level.

Benny learnt the hard way that he had to put some of the money he had made from his houses back into them. Eventually he had no choice but to spend a few thousand dollars on better fittings and repairs. Tenants came immediately and when he'd had time to digest it, he was very pleased.

Buying investment properties is a business, and needs to be treated as one. In any successful business you need to invest some of the profits back into it, and not allow it to deteriorate.

15
Getting finance

Think for a moment about buying something like a pair of running shoes. Wrong shoes can do untold damage to your feet, so you look for ones that fit your feet and suit your needs. You'd probably also try to buy them from someone who has real experience with sports shoes and can give you a few clues as to what to look for.

Getting a loan is no different from this. It is just another commodity, which you should ensure satisfies your particular needs (gives you a "good fit" if you like). It's also best if you get it from someone whose expertise you can rely on and who can give you a few pointers about the best way to arrange things.

Loans, like running shoes, are not all the same. They can be used for many different purposes. In fact, the creative use of finance can greatly improve the returns from property investment. In *Building Wealth through Investment Property* I made the following comments:

> Creative use of mortgages can greatly improve the returns from your property investment portfolio, and allow you to be far less restricted in your wealth building plans. It's most important to realise that you don't need large amounts of cash upfront to invest in property and there's always more than one way to finance or refinance property.

Whenever I am about to purchase property, I may spend several weeks sorting through the options available to me to finance it. Be flexible, and think laterally.

71. The formula

Four years ago Frank wrote to me describing how he solved his problem of always being denied loans by financial institutions when he wanted to borrow to buy investment property. His letter read:

Over a period of six years, I purchased two houses and a commercial unit, and in all that time I could never get any clear indication from bank managers of what my loan repayment limit was. All they would say was that it was between 25% and 33% of my income.

Every time I asked for a loan they told me I didn't fit their lending formula, when I knew from my rough sums that I could easily afford it. So I just cruised along believing I couldn't do anything except sit and wait for my figures to improve so I would once again fit their formula.

Then I started to think. It didn't seem right that everyone was made to fit into the same shoe size when everyone has a different sized foot. So with some hints from your book, I devised a method to calculate for myself what my borrowing potential was. With this formula, I went back to one of the banks to show them how I thought I could afford another loan of $200,000, after they'd told me I couldn't possibly borrow any more. I walked out of that bank with a loan for $200,000 and I purchased two properties.

I hope this message helps many other people to be more successful with their bank managers, so they're not just sitting around wasting those good productive years being discouraged from investing in their own future. As soon as I am able, I would like to borrow more funds to buy more properties using my formula.

Author's note:

When I contacted Frank in connection with this book, he had bought five more investment properties, making a total of ten, and has since semi-retired. In fact, he now spends some of his spare time helping other people prepare their loan applications for their banks.

Frank had the initiative to create his own variation on the formulas given in both my books, *Building Wealth through Investment Property* and *Building Wealth in Changing Times*. I have found you will score many "brownie points" with your bank manager by preparing your own figures to show him why you think you can afford a loan. Bank managers need to have confidence in you. They like to know that you are a capable person who can not only afford the repayments, but manage them as well. And whilst most banks use rigid and conservative criteria to determine your borrowing limit, the onus is on you to show them otherwise.

72. The extra 0.5%

Joy and Ivan have been property investors for more than 20 years and were due to refinance a seven figure loan on their properties. They were in a dilemma over who they should use, as their present financier with whom they had established a very good rapport had just been transferred.

Their property loans were with companies that dealt with the secondary mortgage market at rates of 2% — 3% lower than the local bank which handled their business loans. However, over the past year the banks had become more competitive and Joy had often considered shifting all their property loans over to the same bank as their business.

The main stumbling block at their local bank was the manager. Joy thought he was too pedantic and so wouldn't be creative enough to help organise their property finance. She gauged this when she once received a curt phone call from him to say their cheque account was overdrawn by $11.50, when the bank was already holding their $100,000 term deposit.

But with a refinance imminent, Joy decided to find out if he was still around. She inquired at the counter if Mr Hanley was in — no one dared call him by his first name, Albert. The clerk told her that Mr Hanley had retired three months ago and that Barry had taken his place. This was good news, Joy thought. Not only had the old manager gone but she could actually call the new one by his first name.

"Where has he come from?" she enquired.

"Commercial lending on the Gold Coast," was the reply.

This was also good news as Joy surmised he would be quite familiar with creative financing.

"And how old is he?" she asked more daringly.

"About 45," said the girl at the counter. This was even better news, as Joy thought he was young enough to be not so set in his ways.

"When can I make an appointment?"

The appointment was set and Joy and Ivan had a long informal chat with Barry. He recognised them as exceptionally well qualified clients and they recognised him as an innovative bank manager who gave them some new ideas even at their first meeting.

Although the interest rate was 0.5% higher than they could have had elsewhere, Joy and Ivan considered it was worth every cent (thousands of dollars) to have a sympathetic and creative financier who made suggestions that helped them enhance their net worth.

Author's note:

What more can I say? Look for a bank manager, rather than a bank.

73.   The interest

During the first ten years of our marriage we bought many properties, but it was more of a hoarding instinct than an investment mentality. We never seemed to be flush with funds and to make things worse, we appeared to be paying a lot in tax — and provisional tax, to boot. At that stage, we were too absorbed in establishing careers to pay much attention to money-management or tax matters, and so it was left to Ian, with little help from me, to organise our finances in between working and playing sport.

When I left teaching to have our first child, however, I had some spare hours every now and then and I reluctantly took responsibility for doing the tax and managing our cash flow. But I soon became interested and started to read everything I could on property and finance, for although teaching financial maths in high school, as you know, I'd learned nothing from the textbooks about property, cash flows and tax.

I borrowed from libraries, bought many books, and in one year, I recall, I made hundreds of phone calls. I wasn't really sure of what I was looking for but I found it anyway. It was an interest-only loan.

We had always taken principal and interest loans — usually over 10 to 15 years with a variable interest rate, and on top of that, we had tried to pay them off even faster. We did this because we didn't know any different. That was what the bank offered, that was what we took and that was how we had been taught to handle debt. It took me a long time to realise that paying back so much in principal was the reason we never had any money to spare.

That damn real estate salesman that I had met in Sydney years before was right after all (see Story 57). We had such a relatively high net worth, courtesy of short-term principal and interest loans, that we could have borrowed to buy heaps more property.

In two years we had refinanced all the properties and borrowed to buy more. We also reduced our tax burden, and with the help of Section 221D, our cash flow improved and we never looked back.

Author's note:

An interest-only loan is a hard concept to grasp. It was for me, at first, but it became easier to accept once I realised how much it frees up your cash flow by cutting out the principal payments.

Nowadays, we still use interest-only loans, but we tend to mix and match loans more with some interest-only, some principal and interest (always over 25 years or more), and some as credit lines, with most fixed and a few variable. But the bottom line always is to take the sort of loan that allows you to sleep best at night.

74. The answer is "no"

Shane and Winnie live in Newcastle, and at the time this story begins they had paid out the mortgage on their home many years before. They had always liked the north coast of New South Wales and dreamt of the day they could retire there close to the water. After many trips up, they found a block of land they liked just 20 metres from the beach, with fantastic "never-to-be-built-out" water views. The price of the land was $150,000 and they immediately signed a contract subject to finance.

Shane was a bus driver for the local council earning $32,000 per year and Winnie was a casual teacher's aide making $15,000 per year. They had managed to save $20,000 since paying out their mortgage, which they intended to use as a deposit for the land. To purchase it, they would need a loan of about $130,000.

They had never sought a loan for anything other than their house those 20 years ago, so their financial expertise was minimal. But having done a few sums on the back of an envelope to reassure themselves they could handle the loan, they went to their own credit union looking for finance. They were immediately told:

"I'm sorry, it's our policy to exclude your wife's income from our lending criteria because she is only casually employed and I'm afraid you don't qualify for the loan based on your income only.

"At 7% interest on $130,000 over 25 years, the loan repayments would be $11,000 per year and we will only allow 30%, or $9,600, of your wage to be allocated to the loan. Perhaps you could find a cheaper block of land, which we would be happy to finance."

This was a bit of a shock to Shane and Winnie. They didn't want a block of land other than the one they had already chosen. And, whilst they may not have met the credit union's qualifications, they knew in their own minds they could afford the loan. Shane felt the dream was going to be impossible, but his wife urged him on.

So they visited another credit union, only to be told:

"We don't finance property outside large metropolitan areas, and your own house alone wouldn't provide sufficient security for the loan. Perhaps you could find a cheaper block of land which we would be happy to finance using your own house as full security."

This reply had a familiar ring to it, but while most people would have given up at this stage, Shane and Winnie tried a third time.

"Yes, we could finance this for you if there was a house on the land. Then it would produce rent to assist with the repayment of your loan. But no, we don't do construction finance so I'm sorry, we can't help."

Three strikes and you're out, they say, but Shane and Winnie kept trying, though with the contract on their dream land about to fall over due to the lack of finance, they were beginning to get desperate. That night, they sat up until midnight making a list of all the financial institutions they intended visiting the next day. They also neatly typed out their own financial position and their future plans for the block of land.

Next morning they went to the first place on their list of five. The first thing they did when they met the manager was to hand him their assets and liabilities statement. They then spent an hour explaining their situation and waited with bated breath for his decision.

"Yes, I'm sure we could arrange finance for you. We have a branch office in that town and I'll get them to do a valuation for us. We can even arrange some extra funds for the stamp duty if you like."

Shane and Winnie didn't know what they said that was different. All they knew was they wouldn't take "no" for an answer and were prepared to go to the other four banks on their list, if need be.

Author's note:

Whilst the neatly set out statement that Shane and Winnie presented certainly helped their cause, it was more likely that they had finally found a financial institution which suited their needs.

To mention my introductory comparison again, shopping for finance is like shopping for shoes. You just can't buy a pair of tennis shoes in the same shoe shop that sells men's imported leather shoes, and likewise you won't find ladies' stilettos in a sports store specialising in running shoes.

Financial institutions are all different. Some specialise in business loans, some in owner-occupier loans, some in residential property loans, some in commercial loans, some in construction loans. Some will take a security over any property anywhere, city or country, some won't look at rural areas or acreage. Some specialise in loans of less than $100,000, some in loans of more than $1,000,000. Some only have principal and interest loans, some only have interest-only loans. Some only have loans with fixed interest rates, some only variable rates.

The only trouble is that they don't hang a sign on the door telling you what they specialise in. You have to ask. So if you're looking for a fixed rate, interest-only loan for $400,000 from a place that specialises in variable rate principal and interest loans of $100,000 or less and they say no, then you're simply in the wrong shop. Learn that a "no" may well mean "no, we don't specialise in the sort of loan you are looking for, try somewhere else".

75. Paying the penalty

Maurice is a teller with a large bank and as such, he has had the benefit of a low interest rate on his home for the past ten years. But unlike many of his colleagues in the banking industry, he has made the most of his cheap loan and has put his savings towards buying property.

In 1992, he bought two investment properties just days apart. Even though he worked for a bank, it was sometimes easier, with less conflict of interest, to shop around for the best and cheapest finance. He never used his weight as a bank employee to negotiate anything special, but he did use his knowledge of the banking industry to ask the right questions.

He needed to borrow the full amount of $250,000 for both properties, and the best deal he could get was a principal and interest loan over 25 years, at 11.5% fixed for five years. This sounded good to Maurice, as just two years previously, interest rates had been up to 15%, and rates hadn't been below 13% for more than six years. So he established the loan with this "rival" bank, and was more than happy with the deal.

Three years later, his investment properties were going well: vacancies were very low and rents had started to rise. The only problem, which was more an aggravation than a problem, was that interest rates had fallen — and Maurice had that fixed rate loan. He watched as the five year rates fell to 11% then to 9% and all the way to 7.6%.

Maurice told me he was still pleased that he had taken a fixed rate loan because he would have been in trouble had interest rates risen to 20%, but nevertheless, switching to a lower rate would be nice. He weighed up the pros and cons of shifting to another bank. Yes, there were several banks willing to refinance him. His Loan to Value Ratio (LVR) of 75% was reasonable, so he represented a good credit risk. All he had to do now was to find out exactly what penalty he would incur to refinance.

The penalty was quite substantial. Given that the margin between his own fixed rate and the current fixed rate was almost 4%, the penalty was equivalent to the margin times the term left on the loan. In other words, with over two years still left to run, the penalty amounted to a staggering $20,000. This was no surprise, as he knew when he originally took out the fixed rate that it would be the case. But it still hurt.

Understandably, Maurice was keen to take advantage of the lower rate, but was much less keen on paying the penalty. So he decided to talk to the loans officer to see if there was any leeway in the penalty conditions.

Maurice went prepared. He had statements from three different financial institutions indicating their willingness to refinance the now $235,000 loan with the $20,000 penalty added on top, at rates of around 7.5% fixed.

This would reduce his monthly payments from $2,400 (on the original $250,000 loan at 11.5%) to $1,600 (on the new $255,000 loan at 7.6%).

Deep into the conversation, Maurice pointed out that he was more than happy with his existing financial arrangements, apart from the interest rate. He was happy with the low charges, happy with the response time to his questions and generally happy with the overall service he had received. For several minutes he sang the praises of the bank's services without letting the lending officer get a word in. And when he thought the moment was right, he popped the question:

"What can you do about waiving the penalty to keep me as a client?"

The loans officer was quite taken aback. Maurice was sure that up to that point he had no intention of waiving, or even reducing the penalty, but rather was just working out how to absorb it into a refinanced loan.

"Let me think about it," was the reply. "I'll have to talk to my boss."

Maurice shook hands and left with a parting word:

"I'm sure you'll be able to do something."

By the end of the week he got his phone call.

"I'm sorry," said the lending officer. "I've talked to my boss and we can only waive the penalty if you're prepared to accept a five year rate of 8% instead of our current 7.6%."

Naturally, Maurice agreed.

Author's note:

It pays to ask. The worst answer you can possibly get is the one you already know. It can only get better. In Maurice's case, he didn't use his position as a bank employee to sway the decision. But he knew, coming from the inside, that it is sometimes cheaper for a bank to "come to the party" and keep an existing client rather than pay the associated advertising and marketing costs of chasing up new clients. It doesn't always work, especially with respect to refinancing to lower rates, but it pays to ask.

And on the subject of switching to lower interest rates, there are many pros and cons to consider. I have often been "caught" with falling rates on a fixed rate loan. In some instances I have switched, in most I grin and bear it. But I am always pleased to be "caught" with a fixed rate loan when interest rates are rising.

Switching to a lower fixed rate and paying a penalty has the advantage of reducing your cash flow, but simultaneously has the disadvantage of increasing your LVR (loan-to-value ratio), which may incur a mortgage insurance cost. But if your cash flow is tight and is stopping you from buying more property, then it may be an advantage to switch to the lower rate to reduce the loan payments accordingly.

16
Taxing issues

Everyone likes to buy bargains at post Christmas sales. But saving a lot of money on a pair of Italian shoes, say, is only good if we really need them. Buying them purely for the savings serves no purpose at all.

Similarly, everyone likes to save on their tax. But tax savings should never be the primary reason for investing. We should never lose sight of the fact that we should be investing for our financial future.

While income-producing property may well be *the* most tax advantaged investment (Economic Planning Advisory Council, Research Paper No. 3), it still represents a good investment even without the tax benefits. The tax benefits simply turn it into a great investment.

Arranging our financial affairs in a tax effective way can maximise the returns on investment property. With another review of the tax system looming there is much to consider, but the good news is you don't have to know everything about tax.

After all, you don't need to learn all about the workings of a car engine to be able to drive it. You just need to know a good motor mechanic to sort out your problems when they occur, or in the case of property, a good accountant. You can even go straight to the horse's mouth — the Australian Tax Office — and obtain a private tax ruling.

This section is not a comprehensive tax guide, nor is it an in-depth analysis of any one person's tax position. Rather, it is intended to give you the benefit of other people's experiences in tax related issues involving investment property.

76.   The most common question

I received a fax from an investor querying a section in *Building Wealth through Investment Property*, where I had discussed the tax implications of having different names on titles and mortgages.

As Jake explained it, he had bought an investment property in joint names with his wife but had taken a loan in his name only. He planned to split the income 50/50 with his wife, yet claim 100% of the expenses himself, including the interest. He thought this would create the best tax position as he was the sole income earner on a high salary.

I told Jake that, based on other enquiries we had made at the Tax Office, our interpretation was that the name on the title, not the loan, determined the split of income and expenses. I urged Jake to check for himself and I soon received another fax saying his accountant upheld his claim that the rent could be split 50/50, and the expenses attributed 100% to him alone.

Now, I was pretty sure that the tax laws did not allow it. It has always been my understanding that the name on the title dominates for tax purposes. But I don't pretend to be a tax expert, so to be absolutely sure I phoned the Tax Office. The officer told me this was the most common tax question asked by property investors and that there had been a specific ruling on the matter. Ruling TR93/32, to be precise. This is 11 pages long but I quote the relevant section here:

> Co-owners of rental property will generally hold the property as joint tenants or tenants in common. An important feature of both a joint tenancy and tenancy in common is the legal interest. Co-owners of a property who are joint tenants of that property will hold identical legal interests in the property. Accordingly, the income/loss from the rental property must be shared according to the legal interest of the owners....

In other words, if a property is in joint names, both the income and the losses must be split accordingly, regardless of the name on the loan. So I let Jake know this information. I think he had honestly believed he was correct and I'm not so sure he had given his accountant the full set of facts. It was probably more a case of wishful thinking.

Author's note:

There has never been, and I was told never will be, an official ruling on the reverse situation — single name on title/joint names on loan — where both rent and expenses are attributable to the sole owner. Nevertheless, it has long been accepted by the Tax Office as it is a well established practice by banks to put all loans in joint names regardless of the name on the title, and would probably create havoc if the system were ever changed.

77. The cordial mix

A few years ago Tammy wrote and told me how she and her husband, Ken, were a whisker away from selling their two investment properties which they really wanted to keep, all because of a misconception. Tammy said it all made sense once it had been explained to her, but until then, they had been convinced that selling the properties was the only way they could overcome their tax problems. Here is her letter:

In 1986 my husband and I moved out of our home, which we had paid off completely, and went to live with my elderly parents. They had a small farm just outside of town and were struggling to make ends meet. Ken and I were both teachers at the local school, and we still are, so we thought we could help them out on the farm after school and on weekends, and still do our preparation at night. As we didn't have any children, it wouldn't be a burden to work after hours. So we moved into the shed at the back of their house.

It was a big help to Mum and Dad as our extra hands saved them a lot on labour costs, and we also helped with the rates and power bills. But it helped us too, as we only paid about $20 a week towards the bills.

We were quite comfortable financially and had no need to sell our own home in the town, so we rented it out and were able to save quite a bit of money. We'd thought we might stay for twelve months, but it worked out so well for everyone that we decided to stay for longer. By a few more years we had saved enough for a deposit on another property, thinking that the rent from our former home would help pay for a loan on a second one. So we borrowed and bought again.

Over the next three years we paid off this loan, but we could see we had a tax problem. We were paying provisional tax on top of our teachers' salaries due to the rent from the two properties, which we now owned outright. But we couldn't work out what to do. We didn't mind paying tax from our wages, but the provisional tax took the edge off the extra money we got from the rent.

The only thing we could think to do was to sell the two investment properties, put the money in the bank, and borrow to buy another two properties that were negatively geared. So we went to the bank to make sure they would lend us the money again, and the manager was quite impressed with how well we had done over the past five years. He told us we could easily afford to keep the two properties that we had and borrow to buy at least one more.

But we thought this would still leave us with two properties on which we paid provisional tax, and give us only one property that was negatively geared. It didn't seem to solve our problem of paying tax on our two fully owned properties. After much thought, we decided to put both these properties on the market and negatively gear another three that we would borrow to buy.

We were about to sign a contract on one of the places when we thought we should check with our accountant to see if there was any CGT to pay. He painstakingly went through all the figures and explained that there would be about $5,000 to pay, which wasn't too bad considering we had already made more than $40,000 on that particular property, which had been our own home for many years.

After more than an hour in his office, when we were about to leave, he asked us why we were selling. I explained that we wanted to negatively gear the properties all over again, so we wouldn't be paying so much provisional tax. He asked us a lot of questions to make sure that we didn't really need the money from the sale of the properties and then he made us sit down again and explained to us something that I now understand to be just plain common sense.

He said that all we needed to do was to borrow more money to buy more properties and forget about selling the two we had paid off. He said it was like mixing cordial.

'You get some strong syrup and some water and mix it together. Then you have a watered down drink where you can't tell the syrup from the water. A mix of negatively geared and positively geared investment properties is exactly the same as mixing cordial.

'The tax savings you make on the negatively geared properties waters down the tax you need to pay on the positively geared properties. At the end of the day, it is the total rents and the total deductions that we use to calculate the loss. Each rental property is not looked at in isolation, but as part of a mix.'

It all made sense once we looked at it like this and we went out and actually bought two more investment properties.

Author's note:

I thought Tammy's accountant had a rather nice way of explaining a situation that I often come across. And I have used the cordial mix story on a number of occasions to explain a common situation where people believe that they have done the wrong thing in paying out the loan on a property, causing them to lose all the tax advantages. Their first reaction is to want to sell their property to get the tax benefits back, whereas they would be better off borrowing for another property to balance it out.

78. The credit card

Vince and Margo bought their first property in 1984 and now own six. All their properties were bought either new or almost new, as they are both professionals (a pharmacist and a kindergarten teacher), and they didn't want the bother of renovating or dealing with maintenance. Any spare time they have had, they've wanted to spend with their two children.

Four years ago they began to focus on ways to ensure that their nest egg was protected by sufficient safety nets. With total assets of around $1,500,000, including their own home valued at almost $400,000, and a total debt nearing $700,000, they had never had any cause for concern before. But the size of their loans had been gradually increasing, and radical changes, which could affect his income, were happening at the pharmacy where Vince worked.

So they decided it was a good idea to put in place some insurance measures. Their plan — reasoning that too much cash in the bank was dead money — was to organise as many sources of contingency money as possible. And Margo was given the job of doing just that.

First, at their own bank, she was able to establish a line of credit for $100,000 using one of their properties as security. This was a quick and easy procedure. Her next step was to obtain an assortment of credit cards. She had always resisted this temptation, but with no set up fees and free interest if the money was repaid in time, she thought the cost was cheap if the cards were to be used only in emergencies. If they had five or six cards, she calculated, with a borrowing limit of $5,000 to $7,000 each, she and Vince would have access to a further $30,000 or so.

Their own bank promptly approved a Bankcard and Visa Card, and she then did the rounds and obtained two other cards. But at the fifth bank Margo visited, she encountered a problem — the kind she was not really expecting.

"I'm sorry, but you don't qualify for any of our credit cards," said the young man behind the counter.

"But we have assets of more than a million dollars, and an excellent credit rating," Margo protested. "And no one else has refused us!"

"According to our formula," the young man explained, "your taxable income is too low."

Margo thought he had to be joking, but he said it again:

"I'm sorry, but you don't fit our guidelines. Your assets are fine but your $13,000 taxable income is insufficient."

Pressing for answers, Margo found that a taxable income of $15,000 was the cut-off point. Hence, if a person had no assets, but received the dole, they could qualify. So could a person on only a single parent's pension, even if they were already in the red with other credit cards, and likewise, a working teenager with no assets other than a car bought with a personal loan. Margo offered to supply additional information, but it was obvious that nothing would alter their decision and she left empty handed.

On that same day she acquired two more credit cards from elsewhere, making a total of six, with a credit limit in all of $28,000.

Soon after, Margo and Vince received a "flyer" from the bank that had refused them a credit card, advertising their current rates for investment property loans of more than $100,000. Please ring if they wanted to make an appointment with a lending officer. They didn't respond.

Author's note:

As for the bank — a case of can't see the wood for the trees?

For those interested in detail, while Vince and Margo had a taxable income of only $13,000, their real net income was $38,000, the difference being created by their large non-cash deductions. As their properties were mostly new, there was a high depreciation on the fixtures and fittings, and a 2.5% capital allowance on the buildings. Their first property, built in 1986, even qualified for the 4% capital allowance. This table explains it simply:

Net and taxable income

Income		
Wages	$60,000	
Rents	$48,000	
Total		**$108,000**
Expenditure		
Interest	$55,000	
Expenses	$15,000	
Total		**$70,000**
Net Income		*$38,000*
Non-cash Deductions		
Depreciation	$14,000	
Capital Allowance	$10,000	
Borrowing Costs/yr	$1,000	
Total		**$25,000**
Taxable Income		*$13,000*

79. The swap

Brad is 28 and works as a retail sales manager in the Sydney CBD. For five years, he and his wife Bev, a travel consultant, rented. They wanted to buy their own unit close to the city, but the cost always seemed out of reach. So they continued to save as much as they could, determined to get there one day.

On his way to work one morning Brad saw a sign advertising units for sale in an area he thought was perfect. He and Bev looked at the site and the plans and decided they just had to have one. It was close to Darling Harbour and within walking distance of Circular Quay. But the price of the units was $290,000 — a good deal more than they had hoped to pay. They had saved about $50,000 and would need a loan of $240,000.

Brad thought that on their joint wages of $60,000 per year, they might just be able to afford the loan. But their bank manager had much more conservative views and was only prepared to lend them up to $180,000. He suggested they might look for something cheaper. However, their hearts were already captivated and they weren't interested in anything else.

When they went back to tell this to the salesman, he said:

"Why don't you buy it as an investment? Then the rent would help pay for the loan."

"Not interested," said Brad, declining this second less-than-helpful suggestion he had heard that day. "We want to live there."

Two weeks later, Brad received a phone call from the agent.

"I've got an idea," he said. "Would you like to rent one of the units when they're built?"

"Probably, but we'd rather own it ourselves. We're ready to buy right now so we've been looking around."

"But what if I told you that I think you could afford to do both? Buy one of the units and rent another."

"I'm listening," said Brad.

The agent went to great lengths to explain how he had come across another would-be purchaser in a similar position to Brad and Bev. His bank wouldn't lend him the money either, when he knew he must have been very close to qualifying. The agent could see his sales slipping away, so he had been to the developer's accountant to see if anything could be done to help these two potential clients who were so keen to buy.

The accountant hadn't had to think for long:

"Just swap units. They simply rent each other's units, both receive rent and a tax refund, and both are better off."

The agent gave Brad the accountant's figures and left him to think about it. These were the figures.

Tax implications of the swap

	Buy	Buy and Rent
Rent received		$15,600
Tax refund		$5,000
Total Incomings		**$20,600**
Loan payments	$20,000	$20,000
Expenses (Rates, Body Corp, etc)	$4,000	$4,000
Personal rent payments		$15,600
Total Outgoings	**$24,000**	**$39,600**
Net Outgoings	**$24,000**	**$19,000**

If Brad and Bev bought a unit as owner occupiers, their net outgoings would be $24,000. But if they bought one as an investment property, rented it out, then rented another for themselves, their outgoings would be only $19,000 — a saving of $5,000. The difference, of course, would be purely the tax refund. But more importantly, the accountant thought that they should now qualify for a loan.

Brad was quite excited by the idea, but he was also a little sceptical. So he went to see his own accountant who told him there was nothing wrong with buying an investment property while renting somewhere else — even if the "somewhere else" was nearby.

He then went to his bank. They weren't prepared to take the tax refund into account but, according to their formula, the additional rental income would make it possible for them to borrow the $240,000 they needed.

And so the swap took place.

Author's note:

Brad and Beverley's case was a rare coincidence. I don't recommend that everyone should now go out and swap homes, as there are many factors to take into account.

Firstly there is the emotional advantage of buying and living in your own home. Secondly, care should be taken to check that individual cases are not judged by the Tax Office to be contrived tax avoidance. But the case shows how, if you think creatively, you can do almost anything.

80. Linked loans

I was in the middle of writing this book and had hung out the *Do not Disturb* sign on the door when my husband, Ian, came in. Husbands, and sometimes kids, but never dogs, are exceptions to the sign and since he had a rather perplexed look on his face, I immediately stopped my two fingered typing.

He had just received a phone call from a real estate agent named Rhys with an enquiry about our software. Could it accommodate linked loans and mortgage elimination?

To understand the real significance of this question you need to know a bit of background. In 1987 Ian wrote a very ingenious piece of software called PIA (Property Investment Analysis) which enabled the viability of an investment property to be quickly assessed. It has been very successful, and Ian regularly updates it following suggestions he receives from investors, accountants, real estate agents and anyone else who uses it.

Three years ago, we had a request to incorporate what is known in the industry as a "linked loan" into the software. This is where any surplus cash flow from an investment property is "linked" to a home loan. If the interest and expenses on the investment property are capitalised, the rents and tax refund can be diverted to the home loan, which is consequently paid off more quickly.

Once the home loan is repaid, the aim is then to divert all payments to the investment loan to pay it off next. This plan works perfectly — or it used to. In most cases, the term of the home loan could be reduced from 25 to less than 6 years — a huge reduction, and a huge saving in interest for the home owner.

Many financial institutions had taken to the idea with gusto and had even packaged the linked loans into structured deals, making the "soft shoe shuffle" very easy for people to implement. So Ian pushed aside all other projects and took up the challenge.

After months of hard slog, checking and re-checking and more checking of figures, the software was ready to go. But on the eve of its release in May 1997, the Tax Commissioner made a statement saying that the capitalised interest component of linked loans would now not be tax deductible. Under Section 4A, this method of capitalising interest would be deemed to be a method of tax avoidance.

With no financial advantage, this effectively killed off the idea of linked loans and investors veered away from them in droves. It was perfectly legal to have such loans and capitalise the interest. You just couldn't claim the capitalised interest as a tax deduction.

We weren't exactly devastated because you always learn something even if it doesn't come to fruition. But it was disappointing that home owners who were genuinely trying to better themselves through investment in property were denied the advantages of using this financing technique.

We kept in touch with the Tax Office to follow the progress of the proposed ruling, but it became more and more obvious that their views would not change. In fact, the Tax Office is at present rewriting the legislation so that the situation is covered by Section 51(1) pertaining to tax deductibility of the capitalised interest. In other words, the capitalised interest as it relates to linked loans is still dead, but it would appear to be covered by a different section of the Tax Act.

So having spent months incorporating the linked loans into the PIA software, Ian spent another night dismantling it. Now you know the background to linked loans, you can understand Ian's concern that someone actually wanted them back in the program. So I asked him:

"Did you explain to this guy that there's no way you can claim the tax on the capitalised component of the interest?"

To which Ian replied:

"Yes, but he said it doesn't matter. He says his clients still want a linked loan. And he can show them they will still benefit, even though the capitalised interest is not tax deductible." The mechanism of linking loans, by the way, is still perfectly legitimate.

"But we've worked out that there's absolutely no financial benefit. All you're doing is paying off the home loan and adding non-deductible interest to the investment loan. The net result in terms of the amount of non-tax deductible debt is the same."

I was beginning to think there might be something we'd missed — and we had.

"Of course it's exactly the same. But he says the difference is largely psychological. He says his clients want to get rid of their home loan anyhow they can. But they also benefit by having an investment property they would never have had otherwise. I can see his point."

And with that, I contacted several financial institutions, to find that packaged "linked loans" were once again going like hot cakes, despite the Tax Office's ruling. In another day, Ian had incorporated the linked loans back into the software.

Author's note:

If there's a psychological way of encouraging people to take more responsibility for their own retirement, then I'm all for it.

17
Reasons to sell

In my 1992 book, *Building Wealth through Investment Property*, I emphasised the "buy and keep" philosophy of investment in residential property:

> Building wealth through investment property is achieved, not through buying and selling, but through buying and keeping properly financed residential property. This is what distinguishes *investing* in property from *trading* in property.

Ironically, there have been many stories in this book where people have used the trading philosophy very successfully. Some people are naturally skilled in "adding value" to a property, which they then sell. I am not one of those people. I don't have the knack to add value, or the desire to trade, and prefer to keep all our properties for the long term.

However, for those skilled in trading, providing the profits are ploughed back into more property, and not spent on consumer items, this is a fast way to build up equity.

But apart from traders, there are people who have other good reasons for selling. Perhaps they have retired and want to balance their debt. Or they may have personal reasons. At least property is a redeemable asset that can be sold at will. Try getting your money out of a superannuation fund when you need it urgently.

What kinds of personal reasons would make someone want to sell? To buy a car? Have a holiday? Build a church? That's what the stories in this section are about.

81. The Mercedes Benz

Gerry and Glenda own nine investment properties and are now retired from their welding business. It took them a long time to cotton on to the idea of channelling their money into property. They started with just one in 1978, and it was ten years before they bought another one. They then bought eight more over the next ten years.

At 49 and 47 years of age respectively, Gerry and Glenda had achieved every goal they had set out to, except one — they had their heart set on buying a Mercedes Benz. With their investment properties all but paid off, and rents coming in, they were in a very good position to sell one and buy their piece of luxury. Gerry told me:

"So I went looking for a Mercedes Benz. I spent months test driving the C series, the E series and even the S series. They were really beautiful cars — everything we'd dreamed of. When I eventually found a car that I liked, I brought my wife along to see it. She was absolutely wrapped. All our lives we had driven cars that were never new, never luxurious, and we were looking forward to this day.

"But over the weekend, we began to have second thoughts. There was no doubt the car we'd picked was magnificent. But we began to ask each other the same question:

'Now you've got all the money you've ever wanted to buy anything you've ever wanted, what do you really want — a Mercedes Benz?'

"And my wife wanted to learn to play the piano and I wanted to do a course in archaeology. We realised that even though we had more than enough money if we sold a property to buy our dream car, we didn't really need it. And so, by Sunday night, we had relinquished our dream. Instead, we sold a property that we had intended to sell to buy the Mercedes and, with the proceeds, went back to school — so to speak. My wife bought a baby grand piano for $25,000 and found a private tutor, and I paid $30,000 to go to a college to study archaeology.

"We'd always intended to use our properties to enhance our retirement, but for all those years we were working, we never dreamed we would one day sell a property to further our education."

Author's note:

It is quite often the case that when you can finally afford the very thing you have long wanted, you find that you really don't need it. Whereas when you can't afford it, you want it. For the time that Gerry and Glenda were working hard in their business, setting themselves up for their future, they couldn't afford to buy a Mercedes Benz. But as soon as they could afford to buy one, the idea lost its charm.

82   The new church

Michael and Leanne are a delightful couple who are now in their late 40s. Both come from devout Christian families and were only youngsters when they met, attending the same church group. With many interests in common, they fell in love and were married in their late teens.

Apart from his wife, Michael loved woodwork and after completing his apprenticeship as a carpenter, he went on to start his own building company. Leanne had complementary interests, and when she left school, she studied interior design and business administration, skills which would weld them into a formidable team.

Their company specialised in upmarket spec homes, and they became so successful that by the mid 1990s, they were building one home per week. But they also managed to keep some of the properties, usually the display homes they built as part of the marketing process.

Normally they lived in the display home while building houses in the estate, then moved to the next display home, and so on. By 1995 they had accumulated 15 impressive houses, which they rented through a company specialising in the placement of business executives.

Michael and Leanne were not only devoted to each other, but to their church. And as well as donating whatever spare time they had to church activities, they tithed 10% of their income towards the church's youth support programs, its aged care facilities and its family crisis centre. With such a successful business, these financial contributions were significant, amounting to almost $1,000,000 over twenty years.

But then Michael turned 40 and in his own words, "had the mid-life crisis he had to have". With the biological clock ticking relentlessly his thoughts turned to such things as his own mortality, and he dwelt on the idea of leaving a mark on the world. Sharing these thoughts with Leanne, they decided to build a magnificent new church for their parish.

This momentous decision was also arrived at because their friends, knowing of their large property portfolio, had sometimes teased them that capitalism and Christianity did not sit well together. As innocent as this teasing may have been, it had struck a chord with the couple, so that in selling their assets to build a church they would not only be fulfilling their own aspirations, but also appeasing their friends.

Over the next few years they wound down their building business and sold off all but three of their properties, and donated the entire proceeds, more than $2,000,000, and their time and expertise towards building the new church. The teasing soon turned to praise and they felt a great sense of satisfaction and relief as their most significant project took shape.

However, while the parish gained a magnificent new place of worship, the church's activities began to suffer from lack of funds. Michael and Leanne's regular weekly contributions had been large, but with the sale of their building company and properties, their annual income had dropped from $200,000 to less than $20,000, with a commensurate drop in their tithing ability.

Within two years, the aged care facility and the family crisis centre closed, while the youth support programs were seriously curtailed. The praise and thanks turned to cries of anguish and even criticism.

Watching this happen and being powerless to prevent it was far more painful than the "capitalist" jibes they had endured earlier from these same "friends" who were now just as quick to criticise for completely opposite reasons. First they had too much money, now they didn't have enough.

After much soul searching, they realised that in selling their properties they had paid far too much attention to what other people thought, and that even the construction of the new church was partly inspired by their own vanity. They realised they had served the church and its activities much better through their personal success and, without their successful business and large asset base, were not in as good a position to help.

In 1997 Michael and Leanne made another momentous decision. They decided to resurrect their business and start their collection of properties all over again. They also resolved to tithe 20% instead of 10% of their net income to the church.

Twelve months since restarting their building company, they have seven investment properties. The church's welfare programs are going ahead full steam and Michael and Leanne are now listening more to what they themselves think.

Author's note:

There was quite a coincidence with this story — I had two similar ones to choose from. In an almost identical instance, a young married couple sold their four investment properties and left their jobs as public servants to spend all their time teaching for no wages at their local church.

They soon realised, like Michael and Leanne, that they were in a much better position to help their church by working in their chosen careers, and tithing part of their income to their church, while others provided the pastoral care. They too have since returned to their jobs.

It is probably very common to find people in turmoil over how best to serve their faith — by donating time, or money? One thing is for sure. Selling up everything and donating all to the church does not provide a long-term solution to the world's welfare problems.

83. Fred and Mary

In *Building Wealth through Investment Property* I talked about a very
"young" couple from the Sunshine Coast, just north of Brisbane. I wrote:

Fred and Mary are about 77 and 75 years of age respectively. Every
month without fail they attended the seminars at which I spoke
about property investment. At first I thought they were there for
the evening's entertainment until one night, after the seminar, Fred
called me aside.

'Guess what?' he said.

'What?' I replied.

'I've bought an investment property.' I was a little taken back, for
then I realised they were there for more than the social interaction.

'Good on you Fred,' I replied, and then Mary chimed in with:

'Yes, it's for when we get old!!!'

I know from talking to people that Fred and Mary's story gave a mental
boost to all the "oldies" who thought they were well past their use-by date.
And from the letters I received, many people wanted to know more about
Fred and Mary. So I rang them recently to find out what they were up to,
hoping that people could once again be inspired by their youthful thinking.

And I was not disappointed. I spent more than an hour talking to Mary
and then Fred, and in that time, I'm sure we solved most of the world's
problems. They are now in their eighties but speak about life with an
enthusiasm that belies their age. In fact, they are currently planning a trip
around Australia.

To my surprise, I found out that the investment property they told me
about at that seminar way back in 1990 was not their first. They have
actually dabbled in property all their lives and over the years have bought
and sold many houses, flats, shops, and even a post office, often making
decisions based on their "vibes". Their first house was in Melbourne, then
they moved to the Sunshine Coast and continued to buy property right up
until 1990. They currently own flats, which give them a tidy retirement
income and Mary is proud of the fact that she still does the books.

And the trip around Australia? Funded of course, by the sale of one of
their properties.

Author's note:

Seems like a great reason for selling to me! The fact that they have
done well out of property based on their "vibes" indicates their zest for life
and their willingness to accept life as it comes. Australia needs more
people like Fred and Mary.

84. The windfall

Kerry lived alone in her terrace house in an inner suburb of Sydney for ten years. Her property was one of a group of six terraces that fronted a busy road. Double glazing on the windows and a screen of thick shrubs across the front greatly minimised the street noise.

But several of the terraces had actually capitalised on the busy street location, with three of them having been converted to shops renowned for selling hand-made boutique clothing. So the locality was popular among young trendies who often travelled from the other side of town.

Despite the noise and comings and goings of people, Kerry loved it there, and not once considered selling. That was until her neighbour, Dee Dee, approached her with an offer to buy her house which was next door to Dee Dee's boutique hat shop. Dee Dee had been there for even longer than Kerry, and she desperately wanted to expand her business.

According to Kerry, Dee Dee told her that she didn't want to move out of the street because her business would suffer. And she couldn't buy a pair of the other terrace houses in the same row, as the owners were her competitors who had already indicated they weren't interested in selling.

The long and the short of it was that Dee Dee was prepared to pay $340,000 for Kerry's terrace, which was about $60,000 above market value. Kerry knew it was a genuine offer, having known Dee Dee for as long as she'd been there. She also knew that the real market value was around $280,000. A check around a few local agents confirmed that she may even be lucky and get $290,000, *if* she was prepared to wait for the right buyer.

Although convinced it would be a good deal, Kerry decided to first find out what it would cost to buy herself another property. And she did find another terrace house in the very next street, a quieter street, for $280,000.

By the end of the week contracts were drawn up for both properties, with appropriate "subject to" clauses inserted so that Kerry wasn't left as the meat in a stale sandwich, and in less than a month, Kerry moved out and Dee Dee's business moved in.

Author's note:

I met Kerry when she came to a seminar wanting to know how to use her "windfall" of $60,000 as a deposit for an investment property. "I hope I've done the right thing," she said. I believe she had. When a property is desperately wanted by someone, for their mother, for their business, or any number of reasons, accepting an offer that's much higher than anyone else would be prepared to pay makes sense, particularly when there is no capital gains tax involved.

85. Medical insurance

Graeme began investing in property when he was just 18 years old. He bought houses, units, townhouses, flats and — well, anything that caught his fancy. Over the years, he bought and sold a lot of property. But with a goal of retiring financially independent at forty, he always put his profits back into property, gradually building up a large portfolio for the long term.

Today, twenty years later, he and his wife are semi-retired. Graeme does a little electrical contracting here and there, but it is through his properties that he has gained this new freedom. The freedom to choose between working or not, to have a holiday or not, whether to renovate or not, to build a block of units or not; the freedom to enjoy life to its maximum every single day.

Indeed, Graeme's property investments literally saved his life.

Always very healthy and active, as well as working in the electrical industry he had taken a direct interest in all his properties. He personally carried out or supervised much of the maintenance and renovation work that enabled him to successfully trade and so mould and reshape his portfolio along the way.

But two years ago, disaster struck. Graeme became gravely ill when he contracted a potentially fatal flu virus that totally destroyed his kidneys. He was placed on dialysis and informed that he needed a kidney transplant as a matter of life and death.

Transplants of any kind, as you know, are not just a simple, automatic procedure. They cannot occur just on demand. For one thing, as Graeme found out, a compatible organ donor has to be found. Fortunately, a suitable donor kidney did become available, and he passionately recalls his emotions at the time:

"Someone I never knew had the inclination to give the gift of life. The unknown donor had at some stage let his family know that he wanted to donate his organs should he ever be placed in that terrible situation where death was inevitable.

"And I was the lucky recipient.

"If I had not been so lucky as to receive a kidney donation, I would still be on dialysis, or at worst, not alive."

Being lucky enough to receive a donor kidney was just the first hurdle. There was a second major problem in that the transplant procedure itself was not cheap. Even though some of the medical costs were covered by Medicare and Graeme's own insurance company, there was an initial shortfall of almost $15,000, not to mention the thousands needed for the ongoing associated costs of anti-rejection medication, post-operative treatment, normal day to day living expenses and so on.

But Graeme was fortunate here too — he had that property portfolio. He quickly sold one of his properties, obtaining cash for his year long recuperation as well as everything else. As he explained:

"I could have set up a credit line and not sold the property, but I didn't want to burden my wife and family as I didn't know if I was going to live long enough to pay out the loan."

Author's note:

Most people would have a lot of trouble finding this amount of money at short notice. Many in a similar predicament have taken out crippling personal loans, while others have tried to access their money tied up in superannuation funds. However, access to money in super funds is not automatic.

Although there are "financial hardship" and "compassionate grounds" clauses, applicants have to meet rigid rules set by the ISC (Insurance and Superannuation Commission). Even then, access is at the discretion of the trustees of the fund. Some funds are only obliged to release monies if you die or turn 55.

Furthermore, even if access is allowed, it could take many months for the money to be released. The great thing about property investment is that it is a redeemable asset. It is your own personal superannuation and/or medical insurance fund that you can access at any time you need to for whatever reason, without constraints on what you may do with it.

Graeme wrote to me recently to let me know how he was getting on and he was clearly overjoyed to be alive and regaining health.

Nowadays, I'm a picture of health. I now have a quality of life that I once could never have hoped for and there is never a day passes that I don't think of the unknown donor.

I also very much appreciate that my good financial position at the time of the kidney transplant was because I became involved in property investment at such a young age and continued to invest in property over the next 20 years.

If I had not invested in property and had not started so young, I believe I would now be bankrupt and unemployed as a result of the huge costs of the transplant. This would have caused my family much more stress and friction during my recovery.

I guess you could say that my investment properties were my best medical insurance.

18
Don't lose the lot

Most of the stories in this book are about very average people doing very unaverage things in their quest for financial independence through investment in property. Many have started with nothing but a dream, a goal, a plan, and through sheer persistence and determination have won success. Their stories are inspirational and should offer hope to everyone, no matter what their background, their education, their age, or even their income. Some of the stories are so amazing they have me shaking my head in awe.

However, this particular section is not like this. Some of the stories again have me shaking my head, but this time in utter disbelief. They may well make you squirm and cringe too. But they need to be told.

They tell of people who have had it all — businesses, properties, cars, jewellery, money, everything else you could possibly wish for, and then have lost the lot. Sometimes their losses were caused by greed, at times by misjudgment, and many times by mismanagement. It doesn't happen very often, or very easily. But in all cases it was within the power of the individual to prevent.

These stories could easily be swept under the carpet so that what you have is a nice squeaky clean picture of property investors. But I believe there is much we can learn from other people's mistakes, which may help us avoid the pitfalls ourselves. As I once heard:

"Learning what not to do is just as important as learning what to do."

86.   The garbos

Larry and Tiger have been good mates for more than 40 years. They live in the same street, went to the same school, and have worked for the same waste management company (in other words, they're your local garbos) for the past fifteen years. After work they regularly have a few beers together, and on weekends they always go to the football.

Ten years ago Larry and Tiger shared first prize in a lottery, winning about $600,000 each. Today Larry is a wealthy man, but Tiger is broke. I spoke to them at a seminar Larry had dragged Tiger along to, to try to encourage him to get back on track with his financial affairs. And they both told me their stories. Tiger described how he blew the lot:

"When we won all that money back in 1988, my wife and I wanted to do everything we hadn't been able to afford before. Cars, boats, overseas trips, furniture, the lot. The money just went and now we have nothing. But Larry has been trying to help me get it back again. He's really lucky he's gone on to make a lot of money. But then, he had a head start on me."

I was very interested to find out what sort of "head start" Larry could possibly have had. They seemed to come from the same background and had similar interests. So I listened intently to Larry's story:

"My wife and I did everything we ever wanted to do too. We went overseas. In fact we all went together, me and Tiger and our wives. We bought a new car too, same as Tiger, and new furniture and a boat."

"So how come Tiger thinks you had a head start?" I asked.

"Tiger thinks this because my wife and I already owned our own home and we had just bought an investment property when we won the money. But Tiger and his wife were only renting. And now we own ten properties and I'm trying to get Tiger to at least buy his own home."

So I tried to explain to Tiger that Larry's head start had nothing to do with the two properties he owned at the start. It was his money skills — being able to prioritise and knowing the difference between good and bad debt — that enabled him to acquire those properties. And it was these same skills that allowed him to go on and buy more property with his winnings.

Whereas Tiger's lack of money skills, not the lack of money or bad luck, had prevented him from buying his first home to begin with, and had caused him to fritter away his magical winnings later on.

Author's note:

It has been said that if all the wealth in the world were redistributed equally, within five years, it would be back in the hands of exactly the same people as it started. Money begets money because of the associated money-management skills, not the money itself.

87. The last fling

Jett and Tina had it all — a highly successful business, a huge portfolio of residential properties worth overall about $4,000,000, a small hobby farm and four healthy adult children.

For more than thirty years they had operated a motor vehicle spare parts store on the outskirts of Melbourne, and having a dream of handing on to their children a good collection of assets besides a profitable business, they had channelled most of their savings into investment property.

Every year, Jett and Tina had bought a property, and in some good business years, it was two. They now had 34 properties, mostly houses with a few townhouses, and mostly in metropolitan Melbourne, with just a few in one country town.

Jett and Tina were meticulous about what they bought, checking every detail first, and they were just as cautious in the way the properties were financed — they saved a deposit of at least 25%, then borrowed the rest with a principal and interest loan.

Although all were managed by agents, Jett and Tina closely supervised the finances themselves. Despite a debt of more than $1,000,000, the properties were cash positive, resulting in a large tax liability. But again to play safe, they decided to limit their debt rather than borrow more.

In 1989 they were on the verge of retirement and were looking forward to handing over the business to the children. As they grew up, the children had become familiar with the spare parts industry, so they would have no trouble carrying on. Jett and Tina intended to reduce the $1,000,000 debt following the handover by selling some properties, and then they would retire to their farm on the Mornington Peninsula.

Well, that was the plan.

After talking to a relation who had a successful business in the centre of Melbourne, Jett and Tina decided to have one last fling and expand their business to three more locations nearer the CBD, so that when they retired each child would have a store for themselves.

A $1,500,000 loan was needed for the venture, but this was no problem as there was almost $3,000,000 worth of equity in their 34 investment properties available as security. Three extra buildings were acquired and stocked, and the four children took over, with Jett and Tina supervising the whole operation. After eighteen months, each store was running at a good profit.

But by 1991, the recession in Victoria had started to hit the retail sector and Jett and Tina had to borrow heavily to prop up an ailing operation. Their business loan rose to $2,500,000 and with interest accruing at 17%, it wasn't long before the shops were being financed only on the goodwill of their long-time bank manager, who was quickly running out of patience. To add to their woes, their $1,000,000 property loan was due to be rolled over at the end of the month, but even though housing interest rates had dropped to 10%, Jett and Tina knew they would have trouble refinancing.

So they started selling a few properties to try to recover enough to tide them over. In the economic climate, it was almost impossible to get market value for any property overnight, so one by one, the houses went at firesale prices. And as the properties vanished, the three new shops closed down.

Jett and Tina came out of it with their own house, their original retail outlet, and a sizeable loan. But they were lucky! They could easily have been bankrupted, and Jett knows it. He also knows exactly what went wrong, and in his own words he describes why:

"Our biggest mistake was that we got sidetracked. I think I'll be honest and say we got greedy. We were convinced we were going to make more millions overnight for our children, even though we knew it had taken us thirty years to make our first million.

"Our next biggest mistake was that we put our properties at risk by mortgaging them for a business venture we hadn't investigated thoroughly. We relied solely on the hype of a relative. Our properties had got us to where we were, yet we mistakenly believed that something else would be a better investment.

"It's funny how banks shell out money when you don't really need it and are the first to want it back when you do. But then, it's easy to blame the banks. I guess the bottom line is that we should have been happy with what we had and stayed with what we knew best — our own business and property.

"But I'll tell you now, we're not beaten yet. We were lucky to come out of it with what we have and we figure we've got a few more years left to get it together again."

Author's note:

What else is there to say? Jett just about summed it up. But one more point is worth noting. Residential property is a very stable and secure asset. For this reason, it is great to use as collateral for borrowing further funds to buy more investment property.

But there is the temptation to use it as collateral for borrowing for just about anything — including business ventures that might fall over. When this happens, we can't blame property as being a poor investment. It is the use of a sound asset for a high risk venture that is the problem.

88.   The term deposit

Danny and Lola are a sprightly "young couple" whom I have known for many years. But it was not until recently that I discovered their interest in property. Danny was born in 1930 during the Depression, and Lola in 1931. They courted during World War II and married in 1949. Danny worked six days a week as a builder's labourer and learned a lot about buildings and property literally from the ground up.

Two years later they bought their own home for £1,000 and, with Danny working long hours, they paid it off in a few years. In 1954 they bought their first rental property, planing to buy one as an investment for each of their five children.

In the years that followed, Lola worked at a local factory and Danny started his own company which specialised in renovating old buildings (at a time when not many people knew what the word *renovation* meant), and by the end of 1960 they had acquired another four investment properties.

Over the next 10 years they went on to buy more and more, and by 1970 they owned 30 residential properties in and around the Brisbane area, at a value of around $10,000 each.

Their strategy was to buy a run-down old Queenslander, do it up and rent it out — they rarely sold. A local real estate agent managed all the properties for them, with Danny and Lola concentrating on the end of the business they knew best — financing and renovating. They knew all the tricks of the trade about negotiating deals and renovating to get maximum effect with minimum effort.

They even knew how to borrow money from the most obscure places since most financial institutions at that stage required large cash deposits. Their sources of finance included a gas company, a milk wholesaler, and a furniture manufacturer. In fact, they knew enough about property and finance to write a book about it 30 years ago.

They had done so well with Danny's building business and through their properties that Danny decided to retire in 1970 when he was a few months off 40. He had always wanted to retire wealthy before he reached 40, and his time, at last, had come.

He considered what to do with all his properties. His family strongly urged him to sell up everything, the children telling him it was time to put his feet up and retire altogether as he had worked so hard all his life. They weren't really interested in inheriting any of Dad's dog boxes, as they called them. His friends also told him it was time he saw some "real money".

He wasn't certain what to do, so he went to his bank for some advice — there was no such thing as a financial planner in those days — and the bank manager told him that if he sold his properties, he would have enough cash to last him for the rest of his life.

So although their thirty rental properties had been more than kind to them, Danny was convinced it was time to cash in his chips. In 1971 he sold the lot.

With very little debt on the properties, he netted almost $300,000 from the sale. He and Lola took a three month cruise around the world, and returned to build themselves a very nice home on acreage for $30,000. The rest of the money, about $250,000, they put in the bank to "live off the interest".

Term deposit rates in the mid-seventies averaged 14% and their $35,000 income from the interest on their $250,000 enabled Danny and Lola to live extremely well. Considering the average wage in 1975 was just $8,000 per year, $35,000 was a huge income, and they made sure they made up for their years of having gone without by spending it all.

Today, almost thirty years later, with Danny now aged 68, he and Lola still have their $250,000 in the bank, and with deposit rates at about 4%, they have an income of just over $10,000 per year. They even qualify for a small part pension. Their problem is they are both so healthy "we have another twenty years of life left in us yet".

With the average wage now at $38,000, their income and lifestyle have "slipped to billyo", as Danny puts it, and they rue the day they ever sold their properties. They would still like to do so many things, but they are already dipping into their capital to maintain any semblance of comfort. They would also have liked to pass on to their children the fruits of their labour, but these have now all but disappeared.

Danny says he cringes whenever he thinks about his properties which would be worth around $4,000,000 now, producing an income of about $200,000 a year.

Author's note:

In hindsight, Danny realises that "cashing in his chips" was not the wise thing to do. High inflation provided them with a good income from the interest in the seventies, but it was a two-edged sword — it also eroded the value of their capital. Danny recognised that investment in residential property was a great builder of wealth, but he failed to also see that it is a great preserver.

I could have written a hundred stories on this topic from all the notes and letters I've received, and I still can't believe that many people intend to retire on the interest from their money in the bank once they "cash in their chips" and retire.

89.   The Toorak plumber

Max was a plumber and Irene a hairdresser, and when they were first married in 1955 they had absolutely nothing. Always hard workers, after five years they had saved enough to put a deposit on their first home. Max was 28 then and Irene 25, and the house was a very basic old stucco home in the outer suburbs of Melbourne.

Unlike their friends who were happy to stay put in a simple home of their own, Max and Irene had other ideas about where and how they wanted to live. They wanted to move ahead and up in this world, and enjoy that extra touch of class, so they set their sights on living in a fashionable suburb of Melbourne.

Over the next five years they bought and sold five homes, each one better than the last. Every waking moment was spent either renovating, or packing up to move on.

In 1965 they were close to achieving their aim. They bought and sold for the sixth time, so moving into a large, upmarket home in the upmarket suburb of Toorak. They needed a large mortgage but this, they believed, would be their final move, so they had plenty of time to pay off the loan.

This was the realisation of their goal, the dream house they wanted to retire to — the house they wanted to live in forever — and they spent all their money furnishing it with very expensive, and often imported, antique French furniture.

By this time, Max and Irene were well entrenched in Melbourne's social scene. Irene had made many "well-heeled" friends through hairdressing, and she and Max were regulars at all the "do's" around town. They had many dinner parties in their grand home and enjoyed showing off their furniture to their new set of friends. Their old friends from their suburban days were long gone.

By 1970 they had three children and Irene spent most of her time either at home with them or attending charity functions, which you needed to be regularly seen at to keep up in the social scene. Max worked his butt off in his plumbing business to pay for their mortgage, their children's education and their social habits.

For 20 years they lived a lifestyle akin to the rich and famous. They regularly travelled overseas, if only for short periods, so that Max could continue to work, and their children went to expensive private schools. They dined out at all the right places and they dressed to kill. They were very proud of their achievements, especially as they had what was termed in Melbourne "new money" (money recently earned) as opposed to "old money" (inherited through family lines).

In 1989, aged 57, Max retired. They had paid off the mortgage on their mansion, which was now worth close to a million dollars, and had saved almost $300,000.

As far as Max and Irene were concerned, they could finally put their feet up and relax. They had worked hard to achieve their goal and their children were all off their hands. They travelled overseas, going for longer now that Max was retired, they went to the theatre, dined out every other night and continued to keep up with the social scene. But by 1992 they had spent every cent of their $300,000.

They decided to sell up and move into a smaller house in Toorak. This was no problem, they thought, as the house was too big for them anyway with the three children gone, and the new house they had chosen was still a socially "acceptable" address. So they moved into a home worth about $600,000 and put aside the remaining $400,000 to live on.

But they continued to live the same way they had always lived — if you've got it, flaunt it — and this latest cache of money didn't last 3 years. Trips overseas, this time taking their grandchildren. More antiques to give as gifts to their children, and so on.

When once again the money ran out they came to the awful realisation that to sell up in order to get more cash, they would be forced to move out of their beloved Toorak. But there was no choice. They just had to move. Staying put with Max having to go back to work was an option they didn't want to even think about.

So in 1995 they sold, and bought a $300,000 home in an average suburb, where their "old" friends still lived, and in the process released a further $300,000 in cash.

In 1997, with Max aged 65, and Irene 62, they were still trying to keep up appearances and only had $100,000 of the $300,000 left. Believe it or not, the alarm bells have only just started ringing.

Author's note:

It's hard to imagine that the alarm bells didn't ring earlier. But few of us actually sit down and work out exactly how much we will need in our retirement, to live the way we want to live. The agent who told me this story, and who is a close friend of Max and Irene's, watched it happen and was involved with the sale of each of their properties as they continued to "downgrade". But as he said:

"You can't interfere. People just have to work these things out for themselves — sometimes the hard way."

Max is now seriously thinking about returning to work rather than change their lifestyle or sell up their house again.

90.   The inheritance

I met Abbie at a seminar in Brisbane when she introduced herself as someone who should have inherited a small fortune. Abbie is 43 and I listened incredulously as she related the sorry saga of her parents and grandparents. She was bemoaning the fact that as an only child, she could have inherited fifteen properties. The story began with her grandparents, Ida and Walter, almost fifty years ago.

Ida and Walter owned a fish and chip shop in suburban Brisbane from 1940 to 1970. Working very long hours, seven days a week, they built up the take-away into a highly successful business. Every night when the doors shut, Ida and Walter did the books and prepared the food for the next day. All this, on top of raising three children.

They rarely took holidays but they spent any spare time looking for property. Over the years, they managed to buy fifteen houses. Some of the properties were hundreds of kilometres away up the coast as they believed that one day they would retire there to one of their beach houses.

Sadly, they never got to retire at all. In 1970, and in their late sixties, within six months of each other they became quite ill. Walter died first with cancer and six months later, after struggling to manage the business herself, Ida became incapacitated with a severe stroke.

Ida refused to go to a nursing home, demanding to stay in the house at the back of the shop where she had lived for the past 30 years. So as a compromise, her daughter and son-in-law, Edie and Henry, took her in to live with them. They weren't interested in continuing to run the family take-away, preferring to work at their own roofing business, and so that same year, the shop with its attached house was sold.

For the next 10 years, Edie and Henry looked after the failing woman. They tended her every need, bathing her, feeding her and doing whatever they possibly could. So when Ida died in 1980, it was of no surprise to most people that Edie and Henry, to the exclusion and annoyance of Ida's other two children, inherited twelve houses.

Three of the original fifteen houses had been sold in the past five years because they needed major repairs that Edie and Henry were not prepared to do. And Edie's two brothers had wanted nothing to do with the houses — until they found out they had been excluded from the will. After much haggling, the two brothers became estranged from Edie and Henry because they felt they were entitled to equal shares in the estate.

After another two years of bitterness, Edie and Henry relented and decided to share the remaining twelve properties between the three children. But no one could decide who was to get which properties. It was not until after another three years of infighting and threatened legal action, which was worse than when the two brothers had been left nothing, did they all agree that the properties should be sold.

After fifteen years of neglect, none of the properties was in very good condition and none of the siblings wanted to spend any of their own money doing them up for sale. Edie's two brothers just wanted to get rid of the them in a hurry in case Edie and Henry changed their minds about dividing up the estate equally. After all, five years had already passed from the time Ida had died. And so, in 1985, the three decided that all twelve properties would be auctioned off — in the state they were in.

Now if you remember, 1985 was not exactly a great time to be even thinking about selling property. The market was slow, there was a glut of spec houses for sale, and there were few buyers around. And at auction, none of the properties even reached reserve price. But desperate to sell, the siblings quickly agreed to sell the properties to the highest bidder. They sold for a total of about $400,000, and after paying a huge legal bill, each of the three received about $100,000.

In 1995 Henry died, and just this year, so did Edie. Abbie inherited the one and only house that her parents had lived in all their lives, and there was not a cent left of the $100,000. As for Abbie's two uncles, the ones who had received $100,000 each from the inheritance thirteen years ago, they are both dead broke and battling on a pension.

"I just don't understand how fifteen properties could disappear into thin air. Where did they go?" Abbie asked, shaking her head. "And how do I start investing in property the right way, so I won't lose the lot too?" So I tried to explain to her.

"It's not a matter of learning to invest in property the right way, it's a matter of learning to keep what you've got. Your parents and your two uncles had nothing to do with the accumulation of the initial wealth and therefore had no understanding of what wealth was about. The principles used in building wealth are the same principles used in keeping it."

Author's note:

How many times have you seen an inheritance frittered away — lost by the next generation. If there's anything to be gained by this story it's a lesson in realising that we must teach our children how to handle wealth. That's easier said than done. We are all riddled with those guilty feelings that tell us we must give our children all the things that we never had as children ourselves because our parents couldn't afford them. But we must also understand that in not having those things as children, we were better able to learn about getting them for ourselves. It's the getting, not the taking, that teaches us about wealth.

19
Stories from abroad

Building wealth through investment property is not a strategy unique to people living and investing in Australia. In fact, many successful property investors either live and invest overseas or live overseas and invest in Australia. They have successfully applied the principle of accumulating properties with a view to retiring financially secure, despite the widely varying Government rules, regulations and tax systems.

For example, New Zealand has a Goods and Services Tax, low marginal tax rates but no Capital Gains Tax. In the United Kingdom, as well as the existence of a Value Added Tax, losses on investment properties cannot be claimed against other personal income while in contrast, in the United States of America, even the interest on an owner-occupied home loan is tax deductible.

However, it is not possible in this section to provide a detailed account of the property investment scene in every overseas country as the taxation systems in particular, do vary significantly and would no doubt fill another book.

My intention in relating the following stories is to enable Australian investors to gain an insight into the situations encountered by overseas property investors and to highlight the fact that people can still build wealth through investment in property in any free market economy. These stories should also help to allay the fears of those who are overly concerned about possible changes to the Australian regulations and tax system and their long-term effect on property investment.

91. In the UK

John is an Australian who has lived on and off in the United Kingdom for the past twenty three years. He first went there in 1975 on a working holiday, converting the $7,000 he had earned in the Queensland mines into English pounds. But over the next three months, he watched helplessly as the pound crashed and the price of goods spiralled. He decided that the best way to preserve the value of his money was to put it into property.

With no previous experience, John bought the only property he could afford — an old house for £8,500 — using £4,000 of his savings and a loan of £4,500. The house was in a bad way, so John set about bringing it back to habitable condition, but he soon realised that old English houses are extremely difficult to alter. All the plumbing and electrical wiring were the original lead, the plaster lining was matted on to sticks to hold it together, and there was a bad case of rising damp.

Six months into the renovation, up to his armpits in rubble and feeling weak and tired from eating only toast and jam for months on end because he couldn't afford anything else, he found a piece of paper tucked under the floorboards. It was the original bill of sale which showed that in 1896, the house had been bought for £87 10s 3d! This bit of paper was like manna from heaven. It made him realise that it was definitely possible to make money from property, and the huge mental lift this gave him enabled him to finish the renovation with a vengeance. In 1978, John sold the house for £20,000 and he tells me that, today, it is worth £65,000.

John's first experience with renovating was the start of a new career. He did a carpentry course at night school and went on to renovate many old houses, buying, selling and keeping some along the way. In fact, John was so convinced he was on the right track, that when property values experienced a downturn in the early nineties and people were afraid to buy, preferring to rent, he was buying properties that cost him £80 in weekly loan payments and renting them for £100 a week. With property values now up by about 60%, he has reaped the rewards for his persistence.

John now renovates buildings full time — but not just his own. His experience in renovating old English houses, sometimes hundreds of years old and often with walls three feet thick and horse hair matted plaster, has placed his expert services in great demand. But despite his successful new career, he recognises that it is the properties he is able to accumulate that will provide his long-term security.

Author's note:

Despite no tax deductions for interest and a VAT of 17.5% on building materials, John, along with many others I know, has shown that property in the UK is still a great investment.

92. In the USA

Randy owns more than 300 properties scattered all over the United States of America. He used to be a fireman but has now become a full-time property investor and manages his own properties. He likes it that way. He loves fiddling with renovations and he loves meeting people — his biggest advantage in personally managing his properties. On his most recent visit to Australia, Randy told me how he got started.

Twelve years ago he was thrown head first into the deep end of property investment and was put in a position where he could either sink or swim. Obviously, he swam. In 1986, fed up with never having any money, Randy attended a course on property run by a Chicago group that espoused the idea that anyone could be financially free if only they wanted to be. The course was not cheap — it cost Randy almost US$4,000, and he had to borrow half the amount on his credit card.

The course lasted three days, and for the first two days the class was deluged with information on why it was their own poor attitude that was causing them to live in a rut. On the third day, the group was stripped of all credit cards and identification and sent out on to the streets with just $5. To pass the course, they each had to return by nightfall, having bought a property. It could only happen in the USA!

In the USA most properties are bought with assumable loans, meaning that when you buy a property, you take over, or assume, the loan for that property. If a person has any equity in that property, that becomes the negotiable part. So how does a vendor buy their next property if they don't get any real money? They do the same with the next vendor, and so on.

So this is what Randy did. And it worked. On that life changing day, he headed straight for the local news stand, bought a newspaper, browsed through the real estate ads, and found ten likely prospects. He used his $5 in phone calls and then walked or hitched a ride to each house, until he finally struck gold at his sixth attempt. He bought the property with no deposit, or "nothing down" as they say, assumed the loan and negotiated to pay out the remaining equity in five years with an IOU.

The very next day, Randy quit his job as a fireman and has been buying properties this way ever since. Now retired, he lives comfortably off the rent which he enjoys going to collect himself.

Author's note:

I have often seen advertisements in Australian newspapers for offers to buy houses with "nothing down", but it doesn't work here, as assumable loans are very uncommon, and vendors require cash for their next property. In the USA, the principles of borrowing, buying and keeping property are exactly the same as here, only the technique can be a little different.

93. In Norway

Thane is an Australian who worked as a diver on the North Sea oil rigs for many years and now lives in Norway and runs a business building pontoons. Several years ago, inspired by his friends in Australia who had been investing in property, he decided to do likewise in Norway. Here he tells his story:

"In Norway, most banks operate a one-stop shop for everything — property and insurance as well as the normal finance. So I actually bought my first rental property, a block of flats, through a bank. Most people in Norway own their own homes and tend to stay put in the one house all their lives, so the rental market is not that great. As a result, most real estate agents don't manage property, and I soon realised that I would have to manage the flats myself.

"My first venture worked really well with the rent covering the interest payments, so I decided to have a go at property investment in a big way and I set up a real estate company especially to buy property. I learned it was best to buy property in Norway through a company structure because, even with the top marginal personal tax rate being over 70%, you can't claim all the interest if the property is in the name of an individual.

"Over the past five years I have bought five blocks of flats, with a total of 35 individual flats and in each case, the rent more than covered my loan payments. But just recently, property values here have increased quite substantially and with my most recent purchase, I now have to put in extra money to cover the repayments.

"I can't complain, though, as I've done well out of the price increases. My only problem was that it got to the stage where I had too many flats to manage on my own as well as run my business. So I decided to employ a full time property manager who now looks after my own properties plus several blocks of flats for a few other people as well."

Author's note:

At first glance, with so many people owning and staying put in their own home, you would have to wonder that there would be enough tenants to make investing in property viable. However, according to Thane, the scene is changing rapidly. With the unemployment rate down to less than 3%, Norway is importing workers from other countries. And with further progress in the European Union, of which Norway is not a part, but for free market purposes may as well be, the entire European labour force is becoming more mobile. This new trend has not only increased the demand for rental properties (Thane's have a vacancy rate of under 1%), but has also caused a large increase in property values in Norway in the past five years.

94. From Saudi Arabia

A few years ago I received a letter from an Australian national, Tim, working in Saudi Arabia. In part, the letter read:

I've been working in Saudi Arabia for three years with an airline company. We have a local video store to which people from all over the world donate videos. You can imagine in a place like this, there is not much in the way of entertainment, so having access to videos, even other people's family videos, is better than nothing.

Anyway, I came across your video on property investment. And my mates watched it over and over again. I would like to buy more property in Australia as I know that one day I will return to live there. But at the moment, I only have one. It is my own home which I rented out just before I left. The house is in Sydney and is worth about $200,000 and I have a loan of about $50,000 on it.

My problem is that if I borrow to buy more property, I won't get any tax benefits as I am paid as a non-resident. Is there any way around this? It seems a waste to have negatively geared properties like you mention in your video, if you can't get a tax refund. At the moment, I don't have an accountant as I don't work in Australia and have only one property, so I don't have anyone else to ask.

I wrote a brief note back to Tim explaining that firstly I believed that property was a good investment even without the tax benefits. I also suggested that he should find a good accountant familiar with non-residents' tax if he was considering property as an investment now, as it may save him a lot of money when he eventually returned to Australia.

Last year, Tim dropped me a line. He did find an accountant who told him that under Sections 79E and 80(2) of the Tax Act, he could negatively gear his rental properties and carry forward the losses indefinitely until completely absorbed by future income from either his properties or himself. And the accountant quoted from the Master Tax Guide, 14-880:

A domestic tax loss incurred in one income year may be carried forward and deducted in arriving at the taxpayer's taxable income of succeeding income years.

And with that, Tim borrowed $400,000 to buy another two investment properties in Sydney.

Author's note:

If you are living and working overseas, it pays to find out exactly what your entitlements are with respect to investing in property in Australia — particularly if the country in which you are working is not the ideal place to invest in property.

95. In New Zealand

I met Bob two years ago when I was in New Zealand conducting some seminars. My talks were very similar to the ones I present in Australia because apart from the Kiwis having lower marginal tax rates, a Goods and Services Tax, and no Capital Gains Tax, there are very few real differences.

Anyway, I recently rang Bob to find out the phone number of a mutual friend, and I casually asked him how his investment properties were going. Bob has seven now, but he told me he had just sold two "number ones". When I asked him what a "number one" was, he said:

"You know, on your scale of one to ten. Before I met you I already owned a few number ones — dead awful properties — with dead awful tenants that caused me heaps of problems. Otherwise they're all doing really well."

I thought it was a good opportunity to ask him how the Goods and Services Tax (GST) had affected him, knowing that such a tax was being seriously considered in Australia. I had already discussed the GST with several prominent property consultants in New Zealand, and had read quite extensively on it, but there's nothing like hearing the views of an average investor first hand.

"To tell the truth, it's a non-issue. Two months after it was introduced, people forgot about it, and no one talks about it now. The only reminder of it is that it is something you see on the bottom of an invoice."

I was hoping for a few specific details so I pestered him for some more information on how he thought it affected property.

"It doesn't affect residential property at all because there's no GST on the rents, but with commercial property there is. But many investors over here see this as a real advantage. For while you pay a GST on the rent from a commercial property, there is a "claw back" arrangement where you get a refund on the GST built into the purchase price. People found that they could suddenly get back one eleventh of the property value, which was like a cash windfall almost equivalent to the deposit.

"Other than that, the lower tax rates don't affect my tax refund too much because with interest rates so low, there's not much negative gearing anyway. I can't complain about the GST, especially as my properties have all gone up by 40% to 50% in the past few years. Sorry I can't help you more, but we've all forgotten about the GST over here."

Author's note:

Bob did help a lot. It's easy to know the matter of fact dollars and cents about how a GST might affect property, but obviously the bottom line for Bob was that it was, as he put it, "a non-issue".

20
Recipes for success

Most people like fruit cake, but everyone likes it made differently. Some prefer it made with white flour, others wholemeal. Some like red cherries, others green. Some like nuts, some don't. Some like rum, some like brandy. But no matter what your personal taste is, the basic recipe for making fruit cake is the same. Mix the flour and dried fruit with other ingredients, then cook it.

So too with investment property. Everyone is different. Some prefer principal and interest loans, others interest-only. Some use big deposits, others borrow the lot. Some buy commercial property, some buy just residential. Some like houses, others units. Some add value by moving boundaries, shifting houses and renovating, others buy only new.

But no matter how you vary the ingredients for investing in property, the basic recipe for success is the same. First you borrow to buy your first property and pay it off as fast as you can. Then, when you have sufficient collateral, buy more properties to keep for the long term. Eventually, you will be able to retire on the rent. It's that simple.

The following stories are about successful property investors who each have a large portfolio of properties and have varied the recipe to suit their personal taste. Some are passive investors who have little to do with their properties, preferring to concentrate on their careers. Others are active investors, continually adding value through their own efforts. I trust that in reading these stories, you too will gain the confidence to add your own flavours to the basic recipe for investment in property.

96. All new

Christopher owns a menswear store and spends every moment either thinking or reading about buying and selling men's clothes. His interest in property goes back fifteen years, but as Christopher will tell you:

"I may have been interested in investing in property for fifteen years but I am not at all interested in property. I just don't have the time to buy old houses and do them up. Nor do I have the time to spend half my life at the council or the Titles Office checking out zonings for units. Nor do I have time to manage any of them.

"I just buy brand new properties that I don't even have to think about for a long time. But don't get me wrong on this one. The reason I don't have time to run around looking after my properties is because my time is too valuable doing what I do best. But I do make the time to look after my finances. That's why I like property so much. I have control of my money, but can give someone else control of my properties. Then I can concentrate on making money at my real job — selling men's clothes."

Christopher bought his first property from one of his clients, who was a builder of spec homes in the Brisbane area and was caught with a few too many in the downturn of 1983. He offered Christopher one of these spec homes at cost, just to free up his cash flow, and after having it valued by three separate valuers who confirmed that the builder's price was indeed at cost, Christopher snapped it up.

Over the next fifteen years the builder and Christopher became good friends and Christopher now owns eleven investment properties, all bought brand new from him. Some of the properties he first bought now need a touch-up but he just sends his friend the builder around to "fix it up and I don't want to hear about it".

Author's note:

Many of the stories in this book are about people who are very good at adding value to their properties. They are the sort of people who enjoy spending a lot of their time either checking out boundaries and zonings or renovating, often doing much of the trade work themselves. This is a great way to build up equity more quickly than by relying on capital growth and debt reduction.

But there are many investors who either do not have the time, or it is just not worth their while to be actively involved with their properties. Remember, in working actively on your properties, it is usually money saved in lieu of money earned elsewhere. So you have to decide how to spend your time most effectively. Christopher refers to himself as a lazy investor, but I prefer to think of him as a hard-working passive investor.

97. Do-uppers

If you have read this far, you will already have read about Greg, the young eighteen year old in Story 13 who had a lot of trouble being taken seriously. After designing his own business card to introduce himself as a serious property investor, Greg went on to build a huge portfolio of investment properties. His particular recipe for building wealth was to acquire "do-uppers" — properties that needed something doing to them to bring them up to scratch. This is from a letter Greg wrote me this year:

> When I started investing in property 20 years ago, there was very little information available to the investor in relation to property in Australia. It was an area where you knew people made money, but we all believed it was only for the rich or the well educated.

> My parents were average Australians with one wage and four kids. The area we lived in was a typical underclass suburban area where most of the fathers worked for BHP and the mothers stayed at home. Parents knew nothing about investing except for weekly lottery tickets (they are still waiting).

> Most of my investment strategies have been learned *ad hoc*. I have updated my knowledge over the years, and have gained a feel for the property investment market virtually by playing the game. Books, seminars and talking to other property investors have also helped me to stay close to the right track.

> Admittedly, not all my investments have turned out as I hoped but I have always been willing to take a quick loss if necessary, learn from the experience and move on. There have been times I've thought "why am I doing this, why don't I just sell up and get out of it?".

> Then after looking around at many other ventures I have decided to stay with property. I just have to look hard sometimes for the light at the end of the tunnel. It usually just takes a refocus, like setting up new goals to strive for. In the long haul I have done very well.

> My wife and I have been able to reduce our debt over the years to allow life to be very comfortable. Our assets include a number of quality blocks of units, townhouses and houses that after tax, look after themselves. We both drive new cars and live in a very nice waterfront house.

> This is certainly more than we would ever have been able to achieve if we were just working for wages and trying to save. Although we are only in our thirties, we have a property portfolio that we know will increase in value over the years ahead and provide the security in retirement that should be everyone's goal.

Diary of a "doer-upper"

1974   Left high school at the end of year 10 and commenced an electrical apprenticeship.

1978   Purchased first investment property, a "do-upper", for $23,000. House recently sold for $110,000.

1979 - 84   Bought and sold many "do-uppers" — a mixture of houses and flats — in Wollongong area. Kept a few.

1985 - 93   Bought and sold many "do-uppers", mostly houses in Brisbane and Sydney. Kept a few.

1994 - 97   Worked part-time but didn't buy much property. Spent spare time moulding existing portfolio.

1998   Still working part-time and looking for more property to add to portfolio now worth over one million dollars.

Hints from a "doer-upper"

- Buy near cities with large stable workforce, not tiny country towns.
- Always personally check on information agents give you.
- Don't be in it just for the tax breaks.
- Lock in interest rates for 3 to 5 years at least if possible.
- Have a good property management team but keep a lookout yourself.
- Keep a close eye on maintenance and always get several quotes.
- Keep property fully insured (property, liability and workers comp.).
- Make up your own mind away from the heat of the moment. If you miss out, there will always be another one that is usually better.
- Always check out the area and market yourself to find out the true supply and demand. This may take a couple of days but it could save you time and money later.
- Don't buy with the rest of the crowd at the top of a boom.
- Be in it for the long haul not the overnight dollar.
- Have an accountant who knows about property investments.
- Keep looking and learning.

Author's note:

Greg is an inspiration to those who believe you need to be already rich or to be well educated to build a property portfolio. His own style as a purchaser of "do-upper" properties has obviously worked extremely well for him.

98.   The collector

Digby is a collector. For the past forty years he has been collecting properties, and as I was to find out, he collected lots of other things as well. By trade he is an electrician and a few years ago when he was replacing a stove in one of our houses, I told him he could keep it if it was of any use to him for spare parts.

"Thanks," he said, "but I'd better check with the missus first. The last time I brought a stove home she warned me it would either be me or the stove, but she wasn't letting both of us into the house."

This was a rather profound choice, but when Digby's offsider explained the situation, I understood completely.

"You obviously haven't seen inside Digby's shed at the back of his house. He has more than fifty stoves stacked out there. Mostly uprights, plus a few side by side Chefs and a few built-ins.

"But he doesn't only collect stoves. He has maybe thirty toilet pans, at least twenty hot water systems, hundreds of tins of paint, dozens of rolls of carpet, umpteen boxes of tiles and you couldn't count the toilet seats, stove elements, taps and curtain tracks.

"I swear he's got enough stuff to have a garage sale every day of the week for ten years. His shed is just chocker and his wife won't let him build another shed. So when he brought the last stove home and tried to put it on the verandah, she gave him an ultimatum. 'Me or the stove.' "

And with that, they both roared with laughter. When Digby got his breath back he continued:

"Maybe I won't check with the missus on this one. I think I'll just give this stove a swerve if you don't mind. Unless you want to store it for me."

On hearing Digby's story, I decided I didn't want to become a collector too, so I politely declined. But I was very interested to find out just how he had managed to collect so much junk, or "spare parts", depending on your point of view, and Digby was more than willing to chat:

"I bought my first property back in the late fifties. It was a big old Queenslander on a big block of land in a pretty good position, up on stumps with huge verandahs on three sides. I had no trouble getting tenants so over the next few years I kept buying the same sort of property.

"But the houses were all so damn big that the tenants kept bringing in all their relatives to stay — permanently — and it'd finish up that there'd be up to fifteen people living in each house — usually three or four related families.

"Then after a while they'd want an extra toilet, then another bath, so I thought I may as well do the job properly and I turned most of the larger houses into flats. Then everyone was happy. I could charge more rent and they had all the bathrooms and kitchens they wanted and could live sort of separately but together, if you know what I mean.

"It was fairly easy to turn these big old houses into flats in those days. Sometimes I put a dividing wall down the middle and filled the centre of the wall with sawdust to make it sound proof. Sometimes I enclosed the verandah and divided it into kitchens and bathrooms as it was easy to hang all the plumbing off the side of the house. Sometimes I even concreted underneath the house, which was usually dirt, to build in an extra few flats, and then there was the time I jacked up a house to put flats underneath. You just had to use your imagination.

"I did most of the work myself and all the time I just shuffled toilets and stoves around, keeping what came out of one flat for spare parts for what didn't work in another. That's how I came to collect so much. After forty years and eighty or so flats, you can imagine just how much stuff went in and came out. Stoves, carpets, toilets, tiles. You name it, I had it. And I never sold any properties or threw anything away because it always came in handy somewhere else. My wife didn't mind at first because she could see we were making a lot of money out of the flats, but after nearly forty years the novelty has worn off for her.

"I s'pose I don't blame her but, anyway, things are different now. The council won't let me do the same thing any more, mostly because of the new fire regulations. It's probably worked out for the best, too, because there's not so much demand for the cheap flats now and I've just started stripping them out and turning them all back into individual houses — twenty three in all — and the few I've already done have come up lovely.

"There's a real demand for these old houses now. The tenants today seem to be different. Not so many big groupie families. And people are willing to pay good money to rent a big old house that's done up nicely. The problem now is I'm hanged if I know what I'll do with the eighty odd toilets and stoves that come out of these places. Know anyone who needs any? 'Cause I won't be needing as many for spare parts as I'm mostly putting everything new in the houses now."

Author's note:

I told you Digby was a collector. In between talking toilets and stoves I was able to gauge that he was a very successful property investor who had worked out for himself exactly what his tenants needed. You could say he has turned full circle by turning his houses into flats and then back into houses to suit the varying desires of tenants throughout the decades.

99.   Everything is beautiful

Pat is 73 going on 44. She would put many a grown man to shame
with the workload she can handle in renovating her properties. She has
renovated many over the past thirty years in the Sydney, Brisbane and
Ipswich areas and has played an active role in every one. Her strategy was
to buy very old properties cheaply, add enormous value by renovating
them, and then sell most and keep some.

Pat's story started back in the 1950s when she and her husband built
their first house next to our old family home in Margate — which is how I
got to know her, or she me, as I was only five at the time. And when I
say they built this house, they built it themselves — brick by brick — and
they even made the bricks too!

A few years later, they built another house as an investment — again
building it themselves, brick by brick. This must have been my first taste
of investment property because I was given the honour of painting the
built-in cupboards — I was the only one small enough (I was then nine) to
fit inside.

Pat and her engineer husband were very successful and in the late 1950s
moved to Sydney with their four young children to further their business
opportunities. They built and lived in several properties around Sydney
before finally settling in their home with a view over Middle Harbour.

Following the death of her husband in late 1973, Pat totally involved
herself in renovating properties to ease the pain. At first she specialised in
old terrace houses in Sydney and later, when she came back to Queensland,
she turned her hand to old Queenslanders and Federation style homes, often
working herself into the ground renovating them.

But Pat didn't just do your normal everyday standard renovations. It
was not her style to just replace the kitchen cupboard doors, paint the walls
and then sell. Pat restored buildings to their original grandeur. Indeed, her
restorations were a work of art. She had the fantastic knack of turning the
disgustingly awful into something quite beautiful — beautiful beyond
anyone's imagination, except for Pat's, which was unsurpassed.

She spared no expense, sometimes spending thousands to buy a tiny
particular piece to complete the authenticity of something. Once, she
completely restored an old fireplace, replacing all the timber carvings, the
brass fittings and the marble. All this, when she knew from the beginning
that the fireplace never worked because the chimney had long been filled
with concrete to stop the rain coming in. But it certainly looked splendid.

Pat was not just a director of operations. She did much of the physical
work herself, often working side by side with the tradesmen she employed,

up to her neck in dirt and dust. In one old terrace house in Sydney, she herself spent weeks chiselling the cement render from an internal wall to expose the original sandstock bricks beneath. Another time, she did most of the manual work in converting a beautiful little church into an even more beautiful house. There was no house bad enough for her to give up on and demolish — although she almost did.

One old house she bought was on a prime block of land near the centre of Brisbane. It was so badly dilapidated that when you walked down the hallway from the front door to the back door, there was a 40cm drop in levels, with no steps. It literally was a downhill run. Pat thought the house was just too awful to be taking up space on such a prime block of land and decided to shift it to a cheaper block in the suburbs and build two new townhouses on the site.

So she called in a removalist and asked him to quote on moving the house. But before the afternoon was over, he had talked her into buying yet another old house to put on the second block of land that she had bought in readiness for the first old house. So Pat finished up with two old houses on two blocks of land, which she then set about renovating.

Pat's expertise was in art, not money, and she would rather spend time on her renovations than keep a check on her finances. While she had a lot of fun, she was never quite sure if she had made any money or not on a particular house she had sold until her accountant told her some months later. But her net worth kept escalating so she figured she must have been doing something right. It was not unusual for her to forget precisely how many properties she did own, and once, at the bank, she was almost denied a loan because of this oversight.

Today, Pat is just as active as ever. Although she uses a managing agent to look after her properties, she still contributes physically to their maintenance, driving her trusty Toyota Hilux to and from properties or, more likely, to and from the dump. She continues to buy disgustingly awful properties and turn them into something quite exquisite. To Pat, everything can be beautiful as long as you are prepared to spend both time and money to make it so.

Pat has just bought 120 acres of lantana infested mountainous land with a magnificent view over the ocean. Her rationale is that with another thirty years of active life to look forward to, she should just about have removed all the lantana by the time it's time to put her feet up.

Author's note:

Pat is an amazing person and a wonderful mentor — a guiding light to all who know her. In some of my rare down moments, her enthusiastic voice on the phone is better than any tonic I could buy from the chemist.

100.   The manuscript

Investors quite often like to formulate their own theories on investment and document what they have done. It helps them "see the picture" better — in fact, it's why I wrote my manual in 1989. Five years ago, I received a draft manuscript from Jed, based on his experience over 20 years with property, and it was good — very good. I hope he will publish it one day. Here is an extract:

> I bought my first property when I was twenty and since then have been involved in everything, from buying houses to subdividing land, to building warehouses. The yields on the warehouses are about 14% to 15%, but since this reflects a bigger risk I usually borrow only half the amount. Most of my warehouses are in large country towns in New South Wales while my houses are in Sydney and Canberra.

> I once read in an American book, *Street Smart Real Estate* by Cymrot, that the key to successful property investment is research, location and financing. So I have always done a lot of research with my investments as I believe that this prevents most future problems, especially when I have bought with the idea of trading.

> But my overall aim has always been to keep for the long term and I now own many houses and many more warehouses. The real key to my success was to have a disciplined savings plan and I believe that although my income was not high, I made good use of what I earned, always saving something, even in bad times. A very good friend once said to me:

> 'If you are not paying off a debt, you are in retirement.'

> Paying off a piece of real estate gave me something I could work towards. I went just that bit harder. Instead of Friday nights out on the town with the rest of the lads, I paid myself first, or at least I paid money to my loans, then I had just as much fun entertaining at home with my friends.

> So my advice to everyone is why not give it a go. Sure you will make mistakes, but there is no such thing as failure unless you try. If you can do it, but think you can't, then you cannot do it. If you can't do it, but you think you can, you have a real good chance of succeeding.

Author's note:

As I said, Jed should publish his manuscript. He is an experienced property investor with a wealth of information from which we all could learn something.

101. My way

I could easily fill another book with our own experiences as property investors over the last 26 years. But from the snippets in some of the preceding stories, I think readers will be able to gain at least a little insight into the way we have varied the basic "recipe" to suit ourselves. I don't want to expand on any of those incidents now, or give you a chronological diary of our history of property acquisitions. The following is simply an overview, and broad at that, of the styles of properties we have bought, the types of finance we have used and the methods we have adopted to build our portfolio.

We began investing in property in 1972, but I can honestly say it was not until ten years later that we "discovered" the basic recipe of borrow, buy and keep. Our aim then became to accumulate as many properties as possible to become financially independent.

While recognising that commercial property worked well for others we stuck with residential because, with less risk and requiring less homework, it suited our passive style. Also, we were not prepared to boldly alter a recipe that had worked so well for us. But within the realms of residential property we did vary the recipe, as this list of features illustrates.

The properties include some as old as sixty years, some brand new, with some of those bought off the plan; some are timber, some fibro, some stucco and many are brick; some have a tiled roof, some corrugated fibro, some tin; some are free standing houses, some are townhouses and some are units; some are on individual titles, some are on strata titles and some are on group titles; most have three bedrooms, some have one and one has seven; most are unfurnished permanent rentals, some are fully furnished holiday rentals; some have a perfect north east aspect, most don't; some are within one kilometre of where we live, others are hundreds of kilometres away; some are close to a central business district, some are out in suburbia; most are on land zoned Residential A, a few on land zoned Residential B; on a scale of one to ten in terms of price and style, most are around the three to five category, some are nudging eight and just a couple are at level two.

Nowadays, we tend to stretch the parameters a little and have been prepared to include more expensive properties at the more volatile end of the holiday market. But the mainstay of our portfolio has always been the median-priced properties that make up the bulk of our collection. Adding value with extensive renovations or rezonings is not our cup of tea. But as you will know from some of the earlier stories, we have been involved in many small DIY exercises that mostly resulted in a learning experience rather than a cost saving, value adding exercise.

With regard to finance, if there is one thing we'd have done differently, it would have been to borrow more money. In the early days, all our loans were short-term principal and interest, and paid out in less than five years. We then moved on to fixed rate interest-only loans, taken out for terms of between one year, if we thought interest rates were high at the time, and five, if we thought rates were low.

I still believe in fixed rate interest-only loans. However, while three quarters of our loans are fixed for staggered periods over five years, we now have a mixture of twenty-five-year principal and interest and interest-only loans, as we tired of negotiating every other month when our interest-only loans were due to be refinanced. The rest of the loans are variable-rate lines of credit which I believe to be the most useful tool of the financial industry when used correctly. We have used these credit lines to pay interest bills, property expenses, deposits on properties, cash for buying properties, to mention just a few. They allow us to have money on hand without having cash in the bank and we can reduce our debt at any time. Initially, in 1972, our total assets to debt ratio would have been about 10:9. With our increase in net worth, it now is around 2:1.

Keeping track of the accounts is easy, as our property managers (for all our properties are managed by either agents or on-site managers) send us computer generated annual summaries which are then forwarded to our accountant who prepares a final tax submission. But we always go armed with a list of questions, as I believe it is impossible for any accountant to go through anyone's accounts with a fine tooth comb.

Which properties have performed the best and which type of finance worked well? To be perfectly candid, I doubt if any property stands head and shoulders above the rest, and several different combinations of finance have been successful. What did work best for us was simply time. We were prepared to sit back and wait, and did very little apart from keeping up the maintenance and organising the finance. Value adding was not our style, but obviously it has worked well for many people. Trading was not our style either, but again, many successful long-term property investors have traded profitably along the way.

The message is that the basic recipe for building wealth can be varied to suit. If you don't like renovating and trading, don't. If you don't feel very comfortable with a short-term, fixed rate, interest-only loan, take a long-term, variable rate, principal and interest loan, or a mixture. Providing you finish up with a bunch of properties that allows you to retire on the rent, it doesn't really matter how you get there. There is no right or wrong way, there are only different ways. I hope that from this book you have been able to learn from the experiences of others, to gain the confidence to build wealth through investment property in your own way.

About the publisher...

Somerset Financial Services Pty Ltd* specialises solely in residential investment property. Its role is one of research, analysis and education. Formed in 1989, the company does not sell property, finance, or offer personal advice. Instead, through seminars, books, videos and computer software it provides investors with all the objective, independent, well-researched information and tools they will need to be self sufficient in their investment decisions.

Products available

Book   *Building Wealth through Investment Property*

This book should be the first investment that any potential property investor makes. It is an authoritative, thoroughly researched 190 pages of easy-to-read common sense that may well change your life. The book gives a meticulous step-by-step guide of why and how to invest directly in residential property and covers everything from a list of typical tax deductions for rental properties, to how to arrange finance and what to look for in an investment property.

Book   *Building Wealth in Changing Times*

This book uses new information to focus on why property remains the best investment and examines the resilience of Jan's "do-it-yourself" recipe in the changing economic times of the 90s. It analyses in detail the effects of low inflation on the returns from residential property and also answers many of the what if's that were raised as a result of her earlier book.

Book   *Building Wealth Story by Story*

Some of the best information and tips you can get about investment in property comes from the stories of other property investors. This book contains 101 of these stories and provides a wonderful opportunity for investors to learn from others. Some of the stories will warm your heart. They are about ordinary people doing unordinary things to achieve their goal of becoming financially independent. Other stories, about people's mistakes, may make you squirm. Story by story you will learn a little more about the strategies and benefits of investing in residential property.

Video   *Building Your Wealth through Investment Property*

This 75 minute video is based on the seminars presented by Jan Somers. Although it covers much of the same material contained in her books, it is not a substitute for them. Rather, it brings the information in the books to life, providing a broad overview of the why's and how's of investment property, negative gearing, taxation and finance.

* Somerset Financial Services Pty Ltd (ACN 058 152 337)

Computer Programs PIA *(Property Investment Analysis)*

The company's PIA computer program was developed to help people answer their own "what ifs" about property investment and has been described by computer editor Peter Layton as:

Brilliant, logical, and so simple you have to wonder why nobody thought of it before.

The PIA program comes in two versions, one for investors and one for professionals wishing to assist clients. Both are available for either IBM compatible or Macintosh personal computers. The PIA programs are very powerful, yet very easy to use.

PIA Advanced Personal

The PIA Advanced Personal program was designed specifically for property investors to help them calculate capital growth, cash flows and rates of return (IRR) on investment properties, taking into account the tax implications in their own personal situation. Apart from answering all their "what ifs", it will help them work out their own specific investment capacity and budget. And once the investment decision has been made, the program can be used to prepare the appropriate detailed financial report for the accountant and bank manager.

The program will compute cash flow projections for up to 40 years and has the facility for changing more than 100 variables including property price, rent, capital growth, inflation, deposit, etc. There is extensive on-line help with more than 50 simplified auxiliary data-entry screens, where the variables can be broken down into their individual components. It is possible to compare the effect of interest-only versus principal and interest loan types and to examine the tax benefits of buying the property in single and joint names. There is also a provision for saving files, and there is the capacity to reset stamp duties and tax scales should the need arise.

PIA Professional

PIA Professional was designed for professionals such as accountants, real estate agents and financiers to enable them to demonstrate the financial aspects of property to investors. In addition to all the features of the Advanced Personal version, it has extensive graphics screens (such as bar charts for debt vs property value), facilities for recording investors' details and a host of other utilities for helping investors understand the benefits of property investment. This program is part of a package which includes the three *Building Wealth* books and the video. It also includes a site licence which enables the program to be used on more than one computer within the one office.

ORDER FORM

(All prices include GST, postage & handling)

PLEASE SEND ME :

Computer Program: *PIA Advanced Personal*	$140 [	]
Mac [ ] Win [ ] *PIA Professional*	$495 [	]
PIA Professional – Personal Edition	$245 [	]
Book: *Building Wealth Story by Story*	$29 [	]
Book: *Building Wealth in Changing Times*	$29 [	]
Book: *Building Wealth through Investment Property*	$29 [	]
Add-On price for any book with any software	$22 [	]
TOTAL AMOUNT (All Prices Include GST, Postage & Handling)	[$	]

PLEASE NOTIFY ME:

If you want to be informed of any new material, please tick the box. [   ]

Mr/Mrs/Ms_____ First Name _____

Surname _____

Company Name _____

Address _____

_____

_____ State _____ P'code _____

Email Address _____

Phone No. _____ I enclose a cheque [   ] or please

Debit my Bank Card [   ] Master Card [   ] Visa Card [   ] for $_____

No I__I__I__I__I__II__I__I__I__I__II__I__I__I__I__II__I__I__I__I Exp __ / __

Card Holder's Signature _____

Please send your order to:

Somerset Financial Services Pty Ltd	**Telephone:** (07) 3286 4368
P.O. Box 615,	**Fax:** (07) 3821 2005
Cleveland	**Email:** sales@somersoft.com.au
Qld 4163.	**Web: www.somersoft.com.au**